WHOLLY HIS

God's Call to Be Distinct *from* the World *for* the World

A SEVEN-WEEK BIBLE STUDY
BY JIM FEIRTAG

Warner Press, Inc.
Warner Press and Warner Press logo are trademarks of Warner Press, Inc.
Wholly His: God's Call to Be Distinct from *the World* for *the World*
Written by Jim Feirtag

Copyright ©2025 Warner Press, Inc.

Unless otherwise noted, Scripture quotations taken from The Holy Bible, New International Version® NIV® Copyright © 1973, 1978, 1984, 2011 by Biblica, Inc. Used with permission. All rights reserved worldwide.

All rights reserved. No part of this publication may be reproduced, stored in a retrieval system, or transmitted in any form or by any means—electronic, mechanical, photocopy, recording, or any other—except for brief quotations in printed reviews, without the prior permission of the publisher.

Requests for information should be sent to:
Warner Press, Inc.
2902 Enterprise Drive
Anderson, IN 46013
www.warnerpress.org

Editor: Kevin Stiffler
Cover and Layout: Curtis D. Corzine
ISBN: 9781684345977
Printed in USA.

Table of Contents

Introduction 3

Week 1—Our Deepest Longing 8
   Study Day 1 9
   Study Day 2 13
   Study Day 3 17
   Study Day 4 21
   Study Day 5 25

Week 2—Killing Sin before Sin Kills Us **28**
   Study Day 1 29
   Study Day 2 33
   Study Day 3 36
   Study Day 4 40
   Study Day 5 43

Week 3—A Life in the *Yes* Position **48**
   Study Day 1 49
   Study Day 2 53
   Study Day 3 56
   Study Day 4 59
   Study Day 5 63

Week 4—The Beauty of a Relationship Rehab **68**
   Study Day 1 69
   Study Day 2 74
   Study Day 3 80
   Study Day 4 85
   Study Day 5 90

Week 5—Overcoming in the Hard Times **98**
   Study Day 1 99
   Study Day 2 104
   Study Day 3 109
   Study Day 4 113
   Study Day 5 118

Week 6—True Holiness Cannot Remain Just with You **124**
   Study Day 1 125
   Study Day 2 129
   Study Day 3 132
   Study Day 4 137
   Study Day 5 141

Week 7—There's No Such Thing As Personal Holiness without Social Holiness . . . **144**
   Study Day 1 145
   Study Day 2 152
   Study Day 3 156
   Study Day 4 161
   Study Day 5 165

Conclusion **169**

INTRODUCTION

All my life, I have enjoyed history. It was easily my favorite subject in school. Even as an adult, I love to watch documentaries and read interesting books that get behind the scenes of some of the most important and pivotal events in time. One of the most interesting subjects for me has always been World War II.

I don't know why World War II rates so high. Maybe it's because my grandpa served in the war. Maybe it's because he shared a Time-Life book on World War II with me when I was a young boy. I must have looked through that book a thousand times when I visited my grandparents' house. It was filled with pictures—of generals, soldiers, tanks and planes and ships, as well as different battles and maps. Those pictures and the captions around them told the story of the war to me as a young kid.

To this day, one of those pictures is still etched in my mind. It's not one you would expect. It's not a battle scene. It doesn't have a single famous general or leader in it. Not at all. It's a picture of French army cooks standing in line awaiting inspection. Of course, soldiers get inspected all the time, but there was something about this inspection that has always stuck with me. It was a fingernail inspection.

A fingernail inspection!

Look, I get it. Cooks need to have clean hands, and that means having clean fingernails if they are going to be preparing meals for thousands of soldiers. Those soldiers need to be healthy if they are going to be able to fight.

But here is the thing. As this picture was being taken, France was on the verge of being invaded by Germany. The enemy was near and soon would be upon them. All necessary preparations needed to be made to be ready for a war that would determine the survival of the nation. It was a very critical time.

And at this critical moment, they were inspecting fingernails.

Within days of this picture, the German army crushed the French. Their invasion was so powerful that they not only captured France, but they consumed Holland, Belgium, and Luxembourg as well, and those countries suffered greatly under German occupation for nearly five years.

The cooks may have had clean fingernails, but their forces lost the battle for France.

It seems to me that when you are in the middle of a war and on the verge of being attacked, one of the last things you should be worried about is your fingernails. That's a pretty good example of being sidetracked, of missing the point.

This is the perfect analogy for where many Christians are today. There is a tremendous spiritual battle being waged all around us. As 1 Peter 5:8 says, "Your enemy the devil prowls around like a roaring lion looking for someone to devour." For those who are far from God, his objective is to keep them distracted, living in sinful rebellion and away from the Lord. For those who are in Christ, if he cannot mire them deep in sin and evil and ultimately destroy them, he seeks to simply render them ineffective by inoculating them with a little bit of Christianity. That way he can get them to head down what C. S. Lewis called "the safest road to Hell," a "gradual one—the gentle slope, soft underfoot, without sudden turning, without milestones, without signposts."[1] This means that we Christians, whether we are conscious of it or not, are fighting a battle against sin and evil and for holiness and righteousness.

Jesus said, "I am the way and the truth and the life. No one comes to the Father except through me" (John 14:6). This is a bold and clear statement about who he is, about his relationship to the Father, and about his purpose. Jesus is the center of everything. Everything relating to God begins and ends in him. Leonard Sweet and Frank Viola contend, "According to Scripture, Jesus Christ (and not a doctrine about Him) is the truth. In addition, Jesus Christ (and not an ethic derived from His teaching) is the way. In other words, both God's *truth* and God's *way* are embodied in a living, breathing person—Christ."[2] If we get Jesus right, we will see everything else clearly, but if we get him wrong, then everything else will be distorted and unrecognizable. Everything hinges on Jesus and our relationship with him.

Jesus also said, "I am the resurrection and the life. The one who believes in me will live, even though they die; and whoever lives by believing in me will never die" (John 11:25–26). So, Jesus is the answer for eternal life. That life is rooted in a faith commitment to who Jesus is as the Son of God and his purpose in dying on the cross and rising from the dead.

The apostle Paul, among other writers in the New Testament, repeatedly made clear that we were completely lost in our sin and without any hope of being right with God on our own. But God knew us and loved us and made a way for us in Jesus. In Titus 3:3–7, Paul wrote, "At one time we too were foolish, disobedient, deceived and enslaved by all kinds of passions and pleasures. We lived in malice and envy, being hated and hating one another. But when the kindness and love of God our Savior appeared, he saved us, not because of righteous things we had done, but because of his mercy. He saved us through the washing of rebirth and renewal by the Holy Spirit, whom he poured out on us generously through Jesus Christ our Savior, so that, having been justified by his grace, we might become heirs having the hope of eternal life." Jesus paid the penalty for our sin and made it possible for us to receive a right relationship with God and eternal life with him. We receive this eternal life based solely on and completely by God's grace, through our faith in Jesus.

It's all about Jesus. It's all about what Jesus did for us on the cross and through the resurrection. It's all about us receiving that wonderful gift by grace, through faith.

---

1 C. S. Lewis, *The Screwtape Letters* (New York: HarperCollins, 1996), 60.
2 Leonard Sweet and Frank Viola, *Jesus Manifesto* (Nashville: Thomas Nelson, 2010), 80.

Okay, clear enough! That's what Jesus saved us *from*. But what did Jesus save us *for*? What kind of life does he call us to live right now—every day—as we wait for his return?

That's the big question, isn't it? That is the question that deserves a clear answer, so we don't get caught up in fingernail inspections when there is a war going on.

The absence of a clear answer to this question has created great confusion in the lives of many Christians. It is the source of many spiritual train wrecks in individuals and churches. It is the main reason sincere people who want to honor God with their lives get stuck spiritually. It is the main reason why the lives of so many Christians look no different from the lives of people who do not claim Christ. While we struggle to move forward spiritually, this confusion stubbornly remains.

Among the many important things Jesus taught us is that our mission is to "make disciples of all nations" (Matthew 28:19). That's the Great Commission. However, undergirding our mission at all times is love—love for God and for the people he created. Jesus summarized this by saying "Love the Lord your God with all your heart and with all your soul and with all your mind" and "Love your neighbor as yourself" (Matthew 22:37, 39). That's the Great Commandment. In the Great Commission, we understand our mission and the direction for our growth in Christ. In the Great Commandment, we grasp how it takes place. You cannot have one without the other. Our mission is ignited by love, and love permeates our mission.

Jesus also said, "Be perfect, therefore, as your heavenly Father is perfect" (Matthew 5:48). The call to perfection is a call to holiness, plain and simple. It is a clear echo of God's call to the people of Israel throughout the Old Testament.[3] God's people are to be different, holy, and set apart by God. That is how they fulfill the Great Commission he gave them in the spirit of the Great Commandment.

Holiness is a major topic in the Bible. The word *holy* itself is used more than six hundred times in the NIV. When you include other derivative terms such as *holiness*, *sanctify*, *sanctified*, and *sanctification*, there are more than seven hundred occurrences. But holiness is much more than just a biblical theme. It is who we are and who we are to be in Christ. Holiness is what God calls us to. The apostle Peter wrote, "You are a chosen people, a royal priesthood, a holy nation, God's special possession, that you may declare the praises of him who called you out of darkness into his wonderful light" (1 Peter 2:9).

Kevin DeYoung is a pastor and professor who is committed to a life of holiness. He says, "The Bible could not be any clearer. The reason for your entire salvation, the design behind your deliverance, the purpose for which God chose you in the first place is holiness."[4]

---

[3] See, for example, Leviticus 11:44, 45; 19:2; 20:7, 26.
[4] Kevin DeYoung, *The Hole in Our Holiness* (Wheaton, IL: Crossway, 2012), Kindle location 322.

J. I. Packer was a prolific author and theologian on many subjects, including holiness. He said, "In reality, holiness is the goal of our redemption. As Christ died in order that we may be justified, so we are justified in order that we may be sanctified and made holy."[5]

Barry Callen has written and edited many works on holiness and holy living for a generation of pastors and leaders. He argues, "According to the Bible, holiness is for *all who believe* in the biblical God made known through Jesus Christ and who are willing to be a part of what God intends, the redemption of this present world."[6]

My friend and mentor, Gilbert Stafford, a lifelong pastor-theologian, professor, and preacher, taught and modeled holy living exceedingly well. He stated, "Sanctification is our being cleansed, purified and set apart for the mission of God in the world."[7]

John Wesley, who led a spiritual revival in England in the 1700s with a call to holiness of heart and life, explained holiness this way:

> "[T]o be 'sanctified throughout;' even 'to have a heart so all-flaming with the love of God…as continually to offer up every thought, word, and work, as a spiritual sacrifice, acceptable to God through Christ.' In every thought of our hearts, in every word of our tongues, in every work of our hands, to 'show forth His praise, who hath called us out of darkness into his marvellous light.' O that both we, and all who seek the Lord Jesus in sincerity, may thus 'be made perfect in one!' "[8]

God is holy. He calls his people to be holy. Jesus died to make us holy. What holiness is and what holiness should look like has been something Christians have wrestled with from the beginning. It's been part of the great confusion. To put it mildly, because we haven't been clear on what holiness is and what it means to live a holy life in Christ, many Christians have gone on a lot of fingernail inspections for the past two thousand years.

Some of these common fingernail inspections try to make holiness primarily about what you wear, where you go, what you say, what you eat or don't eat, what you drink or don't drink, what church you go to, what translation of the Bible you read, what style of music you worship to, and whom you associate with.

While all of these issues (or at least some of them) have their place, they are not the central issue of what it means to be holy or the way in which one pursues a holy life. They usually end up becoming nothing other than fingernail inspections that soak up time and energy and distract us from the real issue.

---

[5] J. I. Packer, *Rediscovering Holiness* (Grand Rapids: Baker Books, 2009), 33.
[6] Barry Callen, "The Context: Past and Present," in *The Holiness Manifesto*, eds. Kevin W. Mannoia and Don Thorsen (Grand Rapids: Wm. B. Eerdmans Publishing, 2008), 9.
[7] Gilbert W. Stafford, *The Life of Salvation* (Anderson, IN: Warner Press, 1979), 68.
[8] John Wesley, *A Plain Account of Christian Perfection* (New York: Carlton & Porter, 1899), 43–44.

And we just don't have any time for fingernail inspections! There is a war on. Our enemy is on the prowl. He is looking to devour us. He is looking to devour everyone.

We need to be ready.

We need to be in right relationship with Jesus.

We need to build the foundation of our lives on who Jesus is and what Jesus has done.

We need to live our lives out of the wonder of the saving gift Jesus gave us.

That puts us on the front lines in this great and cosmic battle with the enemy. And, as soldiers in that battle, we need to fulfill our mission, the Great Commission. We need to follow the rules of engagement, the Great Commandment.

We need to pursue a life of holiness in Jesus' name. That is what we are saved *for*. That is what life on this earth is all about. That is our role in this spiritual war we are in the middle of.

We don't have any time for fingernail inspections.

So, if you picked up this book and were afraid that you were in for another round of fingernail inspections, rest easy. That's not what we are going to be about.

But….

If you are hungering for more in your life with Christ than what you have experienced so far, then keep reading.

If you feel stuck and want to finally break free from the sin that's been plaguing you, then keep reading.

If you know your life in Christ should look dramatically different from your life before Christ, and you want that, then keep reading.

If your life is full of broken relationships and all the pain they bring, and you long for things to be healed, then keep reading.

If you are going through a time of suffering and trial and are struggling to see where God is or what good he might make of things, then keep reading.

If you know God has called you to be a light to your friends, family, and neighbors, and you want to be a part of the mission that reaches them for Christ, then keep reading.

If you see that the world around you is broken and full of injustice and evil, and you want to be a part of changing that for the glory and praise of God, then keep reading.

Remember, we are in the middle of a war, and there is no time for fingernail inspections.

WEEK 1
Our Deepest Longing

Study Day 1

Everybody has some food that he or she doesn't like. Maybe it's liver and onions (it's not bad, really). Sushi. Limburger cheese (it's the smell that gets you every time). Tofu (sorry to all my vegan friends out there). Anchovies. The list is endless. I'm not very picky, but I can tell you two things that I never want to eat again: beets and radishes. They are simply awful.

Suppose some friends invite me to their house for lunch, and I accept the invitation. They are my friends. I want to be with them. I also never turn down a free meal. I'm looking forward to the day when we will meet for lunch, and then I hear something no one wants to hear. My friends are going to serve their famous beet-and-radish-surprise salad, maybe even topped off with a healthy serving of Limburger cheese. (Yes, I know that's not a thing, but go with it.)

I would *hate* that dish! Who wouldn't? But I have already accepted the invitation and now I'm obligated to go to the lunch. Here is what would happen: I would probably have a healthy pre-lunch lunch of almost anything before having to sit down to that beet-and-radish surprise.

Now suppose I get to my friends' house for lunch. They greet me at the door and invite me in. Everything looks ready for lunch, but I don't see anything resembling beets or radishes anywhere (trust me, I would be looking!). Eventually I get up the courage to ask, "Tell me about this beet-and-radish surprise that I've been thinking about for days." (See how I could say it diplomatically so as not to reveal my true feelings?)

Then suppose they say, "Oh, I'm so sorry, but there has been a huge problem with the beet and radish supply at the store. They have been all out for days! We're going to just have hamburgers and hot dogs instead. I hope that's okay."

Let me tell you what I would do at that point. I would probably express some obligatory regret (otherwise known as a polite lie) over missing the beet-and-radish surprise, while assuring my friends that hamburgers and hot dogs (two of my favorites, by the way) are great. But inside I would be jumping up and down. There would be a parade in the food-tasting centers of my brain. The only problem would be in the fact that I already ate that pre-lunch lunch before sitting down to one of my favorites. I would definitely be kicking myself for that.

Let me tell you what I definitely wouldn't do. I wouldn't be crying over missing what I didn't want to have in the first place. No one ever cries over missing what they don't want. That is true in every area of life.

When the apostle Paul wanted to make clear the change that happens in us when we receive the saving power of Jesus, he wrote, "If anyone is in Christ, the new creation has come: The old has gone, the new is here!" (2 Corinthians 5:17). But if you don't really desire to be a new creation in Christ, you won't be crying when it doesn't happen.

You won't miss the fact that you haven't exchanged your weakness in sin for Jesus' strength in righteousness and holiness.[1] Instead, you will stay stuck in your pride and remain far from God.

You won't miss the fact that you don't have true rest in Christ. You will keep the heavy and impossible yoke that you know instead of exchanging it for the light and easy yoke of Jesus.[2]

You won't miss that you don't connect with the heart of God in prayer. The God of the universe wants your heart and you need his, but you'll remain disconnected from him and not know why.[3]

You won't miss that your life isn't regularly informed, challenged, and transformed by the truth of God's Word. The possibility of being in union and communion with God will simply be just a good idea for someone else and not a present reality for you.[4]

You won't miss knowing and experiencing God and the things of God as the true treasure of your life.[5] You won't find that joy in him, and you won't fight to preserve it at all costs. Instead, you will simply continue to try to find your joy in inferior treasures that will never satisfy.

You won't miss experiencing how you were divinely shaped in grace to serve God and others in his name.[6] Instead of building his Kingdom, you will keep living to try to build yours.

And you definitely won't miss the fact that you won't finish your life with a legacy that has made much of God.[7] Instead, you will invest everything in a legacy that only makes much of yourself and is temporary at best.

No one ever cries over missing what they don't want to have in the first place. I think that is why holiness is a subject that is often discussed (at least by pastors) but is rarely missed in our day. We don't really cry over its absence because, deep down, we never really wanted it in the first place.

But what are we missing? What is holiness, anyway?

In Leviticus 19:2, God commanded Moses to tell the Israelites, "Be holy because

---

[1] See 1 Corinthians 1:18–31.
[2] See Matthew 11:28–30.
[3] See John 15:1–17.
[4] See 2 Timothy 3:1–17.
[5] See Matthew 13:44; 1 Timothy 4:1–16.
[6] See 2 Timothy 2:1–7.
[7] See Colossians 1:21–29; 2 Timothy 4:7–8.

I, the Lord your God, am holy."[8] That was the standard. To be holy meant to be special and set apart from the rest of the world. It was a mark of their chosenness as a people before God. However, the Israelites weren't just set apart from the world. They were set apart for God. They were to be God's chosen agents in the world for his mission and purpose.

In the Sermon on the Mount, Jesus echoed this same idea when he told his disciples, "Be perfect, therefore, as your heavenly Father is perfect" (Matthew 5:48). It was no coincidence that Jesus said this in the context of how his disciples were to relate to others, including their enemies. The disciples of Jesus were to be very different from the pagans, yes, but they were also to be very different from the religious people, the Pharisees. They were to be set apart from the world but, again, for service to God.

Peter used this same line of thought when he echoed Jesus and quoted Leviticus. Because we are followers of Jesus, we are to be holy. Here are Peter's exact words: "As obedient children, do not conform to the evil desires you had when you lived in ignorance. But just as he who called you is holy, so be holy in all you do; for it is written: 'Be holy, because I am holy' " (1 Peter 1:14–16). Again, we are to be set apart from the world and set apart for God's use.

The same standard of holiness runs through both the Old and New Testaments. It is at the heart of Jesus' command to all of us. We are to be holy! But there is a huge problem. We don't look very holy because we can't live up to God's standard.

Take an honest look at your own life with Jesus. In what places have you honestly not missed his absence?

_____
_____
_____

What is there about the subject of holiness or holy living that tends to make you want to keep it at a distance?

_____
_____
_____

---

8 See also Leviticus 11:44–45; 20:7.

What does it mean for you to *be holy* in Jesus, but also to have to *pursue holiness* each day? Does that scare you or inspire you or both? Why?

What I'm hearing God say to me

Study Day 2

Let's be clear. God demands our holiness. God's diagnosis is that we are not holy, and we can't live up to his demand. We are stained by sin. And God's cure is Jesus. On the cross, Jesus took the punishment for sin that we deserved. He gave his life so we could have life. His holiness is given to us by grace. Jesus was *perfect for us*. Now, for all who are in Christ by faith, Jesus lives in us. We are covered in Jesus' righteousness and holiness. His holiness and love flow in and out of us more and more by the power of the Holy Spirit. Jesus is *perfect in us*.

This means that holiness is both *positional* and *progressive*. It is something given to us as part of the gift of salvation in Jesus. In God's eyes, we are holy in Christ. But holiness is also something we must fight to make visible with our surrendered will and obedience. All of our feelings, thoughts, and actions are brought into conformity with Jesus' qualities of holiness more and more as we walk with him and depend on the Holy Spirit's power.

I know this is hard to grasp. How can you *be* something and still have to grow *into* it at the same time? That doesn't seem to make sense. Perhaps an analogy might help.

A doctor will tell you that a woman becomes pregnant at the moment of conception. We also know that the average length of a pregnancy is 280 days. That said, there is no such thing as being partially pregnant. No one breaks out fractions from elementary school to describe a woman as 63/280 pregnant. (Not even the biggest math nerds would do that.) At the same time, however, a woman clearly becomes more and more pregnant with each passing day. Her symptoms become more acute and the baby growing inside her becomes more and more visible to others. She is always and never stops being completely pregnant from the time of conception until the baby's birth, yet with the passage of time she becomes more and more visibly pregnant up until the moment the baby is actually born.[1]

That is how holiness works.

The moment we surrender our lives in faith to Jesus Christ and trust that in his grace and mercy our sin is paid for, we are his. The old owner of our lives—the power of sin—is now dead. The new owner of our lives—Jesus—is now in control. We belong to him completely. It is God's definitive work in us through Jesus. It is by grace.

The Bible says that those who are in Christ are called to be God's holy people or "saints."[2] In fact, the word *saints* literally means "holy ones," and that is what we

---

[1] Idea borrowed from Keith M. Davenport, "Sanctification as Prescription," in *Conversations on Holiness*, ed. Keith M. Davenport (Kansas City: Beacon Hill Press, 2013), 25–26.
[2] See Romans 1:7; 1 Corinthians 1:2.

become the moment we are saved. Paul described it like this: "Since, then, you have been raised with Christ, set your hearts on things above, where Christ is, seated at the right hand of God. Set your minds on things above, not on earthly things. For you died, and your life is now hidden with Christ in God" (Colossians 3:1–3).

God is absolutely holy and righteous. We are not. Apart from Christ, we are spiritually dead and separated from God because of our sin. How many sins and what type of sins doesn't matter. What matters is that we are dead, and we can't make ourselves alive. Running from God and avoiding him doesn't make us alive. Trying to do good things and avoid bad things doesn't make us alive either. We are dead and totally removed from God's holiness.

Jesus makes us alive in two ways. First, he forgives our sin because he paid for it through his death on the cross. Second, he fills us with the Holy Spirit through his resurrection power. When we surrender our lives to Jesus, we are made alive in him by grace alone, through faith alone, in Christ alone. It's the only way to make our dead spirit, soul, and body alive again.

Now we are "hidden with Christ in God." We aren't helped so that we can somehow make it on our own. We are made alive and are spiritually united with Christ. When we surrender our lives to Jesus, we instantly become his. Now we are holy and righteous in Christ.[3] We belong to him. Outwardly, we are the same. Inwardly, we are brand new. We have a transformed heart, mind, and will. We are alive and holy now because we are in Christ. The old is out and going out, and the new is in and coming in.

On the one hand, when our lives are "hidden with Christ in God," we *are* holy as a gift. We are spiritually alive and belong to Jesus. Our heart is now formed in him, which changes the desires of our heart. We love Jesus, and we love what he loves. Our mind is now transformed, so that we increasingly see the world as Jesus does. Our thoughts and values change to reflect his. Our will is now conformed in Christ, too, which creates a posture of surrender before him. We want to obey Jesus even when it's hard.

On the other hand, because our lives are "hidden with Christ in God," we *fight for a life of holiness* every day. There is a daily battle to take on visibly who we already are in Christ spiritually. It's a fight to kill sin, and it's a fight to live out the holiness of Jesus in real and practical ways. As long as we are in Christ, we are holy, but each day we must seek God for the wisdom and power we need in this fight for holiness, so that our manner of life may be worthy of the Lord and entirely pleasing to him. By doing this, we will look more and more like Jesus until he comes.

Paul explained what this fight looks like in the remainder of Colossians 3, writing, "Put to death, therefore, whatever belongs to your earthly nature" (Colossians 3:5).

---

[3] There are other places where the Bible describes holiness (sanctification) as a completed work: e.g., 1 Corinthians 6:11; Hebrews 9:13–14; 10:10; 13:12.

Putting something to death means killing it. Paul then listed a number of examples of the old, sinful ways that once controlled us: "sexual immorality, impurity, lust, evil desires and greed, which is idolatry" and also "anger, rage, malice, slander, and filthy language" (Colossians 3:5, 8). These things hurt us and others. They once separated us from God, but these old, sinful ways no longer fit. We don't want them. Our hearts, minds, and wills are now more and more resistant to them. That's why we fight to kill all that remains whenever we are made aware of it. Because we are now "hidden with Christ in God," we have the power to do so.

Killing is only half of the fight for holiness. Paul also called us to "put on" something new because we are "God's chosen people, holy and dearly loved" (Colossians 3:12). Like new clothes, we are to put on the marks of the holy people we are in Christ. Paul listed virtues describing the new, holy ways that please God, including "compassion, kindness, humility, gentleness and patience," bearing with people and forgiving them, demonstrating love, unity, peace, and thankfulness, and doing everything for God's glory (Colossians 3:12–17). These things build us up. They build others up and point them to Christ. Our hearts, minds, and wills now long for these things more and more. That is why we fight to put them on. Because we are now "hidden with Christ in God," we have the power to do so.

Describe how you would compare your life of being holy and pursuing holiness to the pregnancy analogy.

_____

_____

_____

Looking at Colossians 3, where have you seen this "putting to death" and "putting on" in your own life? How much of it has it been a one-time decision for you and how much has been an ongoing fight?

_____

_____

_____

In what specific areas have you been resisting God's work to "put to death" or "put on" something in your life?

_____

_____

_____

What I'm hearing God say to me

Study Day 3

Now, more and more, we take on the character of Jesus. We become the kind of people who would do the things Jesus would do and say the things Jesus would say if he were walking among us. We do this because he is alive in our hearts by faith. The Holy Spirit gives us the power to actually fight the fights and win the battles to make visible who we already are in Christ. That is what John meant when he wrote, "Dear friends, now we are children of God, and what we will be has not yet been made known. But we know that when Christ appears, we shall be like him, for we shall see him as he is. All who have this hope in him purify themselves, just as he is pure" (1 John 3:2–3). Because we belong to Jesus and because the Holy Spirit's power is living and working in us, we can be like him. As theologian J. I. Packer argued,

> Holiness is a matter of both action and motivation, conduct and character, divine grace and human effort, obedience and creativity, submission and initiative, consecration to God and commitment to people, self-discipline and self-giving, righteousness and love…. In reality, holiness is the goal of our redemption. As Christ died in order that we may be justified, so we are justified in order that we may be sanctified and made holy.[1]

Because we are holy in Christ, holiness is the deepest longing of our hearts. Holiness is what we fight for every day. In that way, as Christians, becoming more and more holy in Jesus is our reason for being.

If this is true, then we can offer a clear and simple definition of holiness: *Holiness is the work of God in us whereby Jesus takes full ownership of our lives, purifies us from sin, and sets us apart for his service.* In so doing, we are made holy to be wholly his. That is why, over and over again, the Bible declares that we are both holy and *becoming* holy in Christ. Holiness (or sanctification) is by grace, yet it is something we must fight for.

This work of God produces in us what Packer called "awed adoration."[2] If you want God's holiness in your life, then you want this "awed adoration." And when it's not present, you miss it. You cry over its absence because you long for it. And you fight with all your heart, mind, soul, and strength to have it or to have it back. Here are some of the ways it looks:

You have a growing gratitude for the mercy and grace of God. Awed adoration is linked to a growing appreciation for and experience of God's mercy and grace, not some kind of religious attitude or practice. You know it's all about what God did for us in Christ. So, you have a greater awareness of your need for God's

---

[1] Packer, 29, 34.
[2] Ibid., 68.

mercy and grace to cover your sin. This leads to a greater humility and dependence on him now than even when you were first saved.

When God's mercy and grace become more real and alive in your life, it shows in the attitude of your worship. You worship God knowing that you are his child, adopted by your precious "*Abba*, Father."[3] You know that you deserved nothing, but because of Jesus you have a new law that grounds you in the spirit of life and not the old way of sin and death.[4] Now you live in the reality that no person can condemn you for your sins because Jesus saves you. You know you don't save yourself, but instead trust in his goodness. More importantly, you know that Satan can't condemn you for your sins because Jesus has power over sin and death. The reality of this mercy and grace changes everything. With the new mind, new spirit, and new life you have received in Jesus, you naturally worship in the reality that you are fully known and also truly loved by God. There is nothing you could ever do to merit being his child, which radically humbles you. However, at the same time, you know there is nothing you need that you haven't received from Jesus, which radically affirms you.

You are awestruck at the awesomeness and glory of God. In the Bible, God's glory has a sense of heaviness to it. That is why there are earthquakes when it shows up. Things are shaken. That was true for Moses and the Israelites at Mt. Sinai. It was true for Isaiah in the temple. It was true at the moment Jesus died on the cross and Jerusalem was rocked. It was even true when the power of God showed up following a season of prayer in the early Jerusalem church. God is heavy, not light.

If you believe in God but it just hasn't changed you very much, then God is probably too "light" to you. Perhaps you are trying to shape him, to fit him around your existing patterns. He doesn't rock you. A light God doesn't change your beliefs, your politics, your family, or the direction of your life. At best, a light God just helps you feel better about your personal goals and agendas. A light God is empty.

If God is "heavy," then he shapes you. *You* fit around *him*. If you truly know God, you can remember when he went from light to heavy: God rocked you! The details may be different from person to person, but you acknowledged Jesus as Lord. He contradicted your old patterns, reoriented your beliefs, and rearranged your whole life. A heavy God like that is real and worthy of all glory. You know that he is so big, and you are so small. As a result, you are absolutely awestruck by him.

You are zealous for Jesus to purify your heart and life. Awed adoration leaves you with no doubt that Jesus is the purifier and that you need to be purified. When you experience that purification, you want it more and more. Jesus said, "Blessed are the pure in heart, for they will see God" (Matthew 5:8). He granted you new

---

3 See Romans 8:15–17.
4 See Romans 8:1–2.

vision. Now you are able to increasingly see the world, including yourself, through the eyes of Jesus. At the same time, you are increasingly able to discern the voice of the Holy Spirit, especially as he speaks to you through the Scriptures. In short, you are developing a pure heart.

God is now purifying you with Jesus' own holiness. That is what Jesus made possible when he took your place on the cross and received the just punishment for your sin. Now God's promise is that you will "see" him. To "see" God means to experience the glory of God. Jesus lives in you, and his purity grows out of your changed heart by the power of the Holy Spirit. You are able to see God, to know him, to experience him, to enjoy him. And once you get a taste of this, you become zealous for more.

Where do you see gratitude growing in your life over what God has done or is doing?

_____
_____
_____

Where have you been rocked by God being so "heavy" that his glory shook you?

_____
_____
_____

In what areas have you seen God purify your attitudes, thoughts, or actions?

_____
_____
_____

What I'm hearing God say to me

Study Day 4

Here are some more ways the "awed adoration" of God looks as his holiness is manifest in your life.

You hunger and thirst for the righteousness of God. Awed adoration will change what you hunger and thirst after. Before coming to Christ, everyone has distorted hungers. You and I are no exception. Distorted hungers are idols (idols are false gods, which we'll talk more about during Week 2), and everyone's distorted hunger is different. For one person, it's some kind of power or wealth. For another, it's pleasure or a perfect mate. Still others want fame or beauty. Even having a perfect reputation or a pristine family can be a false hunger. Idols can be anything, and they have been everything. An idol is often a good thing that we want, but we begin to want it so much that it becomes a competing love, replacing God as our ultimate love. Before we know it, that hunger—even for something good—becomes so distorted that food is turned to gluttony, love is turned to lust, ambition is turned to greed and selfishness, and being physically fit is turned to vanity.

Before coming to Christ, all of us, in one way or another, hungered for sin. Augustine, an early Christian theologian, wrote a spiritual autobiography called *Confessions* that vividly described sin's hold on him and, by extension, on all of us. In one part, Augustine told of a time when he and some young friends stole a neighbor's pears as a prank. They weren't driven by hunger or poverty. In fact, he had his own pears and they tasted better. He and his friends didn't even enjoy what they stole, and they ended up throwing the pears to the pigs. Augustine took the pears because he wanted to do something he knew he shouldn't, just because he could.[1] No one is immune to that kind of hunger. If you don't know this, you don't know your own heart. There's a part of each of us that hungers for sin simply because it makes us feel powerful, if only for a moment.

In contrast to all of these distorted hungers or blatant hungers for sin, Jesus said, "Blessed are those who hunger and thirst for righteousness, for they will be filled" (Matthew 5:6). People who hunger and thirst are in dire need. They will perish if they are not filled—think starvation and dehydration. There is a sense of passion and desperation in this hunger and thirst. You are passionate because all of your body's energies are being devoted to it. You are desperate because you know your life depends on it.

Jesus knows that everyone hungers and thirsts after something. This hunger and thirst drives your life. That is why Jesus said those who belong to him finally know where their true hunger and thirst lies. They want God's justice and not their own.

---
1 See Saint Augustine, *Confessions* (New York: Penguin Books, 1961), 43–53.

They want God's salvation and not their own. They want God's holiness and not their own.

Now, in Christ, our new hunger and thirst boils down to a deep and enduring desire for the righteousness of Jesus. That means we want Jesus' will and way over everything else more and more. Nothing else will satisfy. We come to see Jesus for who he really is. We know he willingly gave up his life for us. He knows and understands us and comes to us with outstretched arms of forgiveness and love.

When you come to know this Jesus, you savor him. In Christ, you have new taste buds on your soul's tongue. As a result, you crave Jesus more and more rather than experiencing the old desire for sin. Sin just doesn't taste good anymore, but Jesus does. So you desire to talk the way he talks, think the way he thinks, act the way he acts, and love the way he loves. Hungering and thirsting for righteousness means you find Jesus so valuable that you would have him at the cost of anything.

You want Jesus to be your ultimate treasure and joy. Awed adoration means to take joy in the right treasure. Jesus said, "The kingdom of heaven is like treasure hidden in a field. When a man found it, he hid it again, and then in his joy went and sold all he had and bought that field" (Matthew 13:44). The treasure Jesus referred to is a life found in him, where you discover him to be your ultimate joy.

One of the most difficult spiritual lessons you will ever learn is that God cares far more about your holiness than he does about your happiness. Earthly happiness isn't bad, but it can never be our treasure because it can never produce lasting joy. Either we will never be as happy as we want to be or we will achieve what we long for but then find that it doesn't measure up to our expectations. That is why it is so critical for your character to be formed in Christ and for you to find your ultimate treasure in God. That treasure is your joy. Joy in God means happiness in God and in the things of God.

Do you feel loved by God because he makes much of you or because God frees you to make much of him forever?[2] Your response to this question will determine whether your life will be submitted to the authority of God's Word or not, especially when it convicts you of sin or calls you to sacrifice something important. It will determine who has control of your heart, because if your heart belongs to Jesus, you will take great joy in living thankfully for him. You will fight for joy in Christ even if it costs you everything. You won't let yourself be squeezed into the mold of this world because you want to be shaped by Jesus instead. Most of all, you will want Jesus to inhabit every part of your life.

This kind of treasure does not come easy. The fight for joy is not a fight for more comfort, prosperity, or security. That's the treasure of your old life, but now you have

---

[2] Adapted from John Piper, *Brothers, We Are Not Professionals* (Nashville: B&H Publishing Group, 2013), Kindle locations 309 and 320.

found the only treasure that truly satisfies. Now your fight for joy is to deny yourself and take up your cross daily and follow Jesus.³ You can do that now because you have his strength. Now you can gain your life by losing it.⁴ As a result, your new life will have inconvenience rather than comfort, sacrifice rather than prosperity, and trial rather than security. But make no mistake: You will have God! He will be your treasure and joy. That is why you fight this fight every day in order to have him.

In what ways has the Holy Spirit changed the things your heart hungers and thirsts for?

_____

_____

_____

How has the source of your joy changed, and what has been the result?

_____

_____

_____

---

3 See Luke 9:23.
4 See Luke 9:24.

What I'm hearing God say to me

Study Day 5

A deep thinker and writer on the subject of holiness from the nineteenth century, Bishop J. C. Ryle, wrote, "Most men hope to go to heaven when they die; but few, it may be feared, take the trouble to consider whether they would enjoy heaven if they got there."[1] Followers of Jesus Christ can look forward to the new heaven and new earth, a place of perfect holiness and righteousness under his full reign.[2] All of life for you and me right now is preparation for that eternal life. When we long for the holiness of Jesus to be found in us, we long for that reality. When we pursue God with awed adoration, we long for that reality.

Holiness is not reproducible in laboratory conditions. There is no formula where you add this, take away that, wait for a certain amount of time, and then *voila*—holiness! Holiness is found only in real-world conditions. It is in real-life situations where our hearts are formed, our minds are transformed, and our wills are conformed to Christ. In that way we can see it, hear it, smell it, and feel it.[3] For example:

- Holiness looks like a retired man investing in an elementary-school boy who has no father.
- Holiness looks like a husband and wife forgiving and reconciling after a fight in which both of them lost their cool.
- Holiness sounds like a mom and dad crying out to God on behalf of their teenage daughter, whom they want to find Christ.
- Holiness sounds like a man speaking gently, kindly, and with patience to others, unlike the angry, ugly, and critical way he did before, because he is fighting, with the Spirit's help, to change the way he speaks.
- Holiness smells like a Thanksgiving dinner served to co-workers and neighbors who have no family in town to be with.
- Holiness smells like a clean house and freshly baked muffins that were just finished by a life group for when one of their members comes home from the hospital with her new baby.
- Holiness feels like the touch of a woman who visits Alzheimer's patients who will never remember that she was there.
- Holiness feels like the gentle care of a nurse who pours herself into her patients as if they were family or close friends.

---

1 J. C. Ryle, *Holiness* (Louisville: GLH Publishing, 1877), 26.
2 The best picture of this blessed hope can be found in Revelation 21–22.
3 Idea borrowed from Deidre Browner Latz, "The Dynamic of Holiness," in *Conversations on Holiness*, 15–19.

Remember, no one ever cries over missing what they don't want to have in the first place. This means that wherever the holiness of Jesus is not present in us, we should miss it. Not only that, but we should also eagerly desire to have it to the full. Our lives should more and more reflect the words of hymn writer Charles Wesley expressing the change Jesus made in his life:

> Long my imprisoned spirit lay
> Fast bound in sin and nature's night.
> Thine eye diffused a quickening ray;
> I woke—the dungeon flamed with light!
> My chains fell off, my heart was free,
> I rose, went forth, and followed Thee.
>
> No condemnation now I dread:
> Jesus, and all in Him, is mine!
> Alive in Him, my living Head,
> And clothed in righteousness divine,
> Bold I approach the eternal throne,
> And claim the crown, through Christ my own.
>
> Amazing love! How can it be
> That Thou my God, shouldst die for me![4]

If we had experienced the holiness and love of Jesus and then lost it, we would definitely miss it. If we never had it but encountered it for the first time, we would do anything to have it for ourselves.

If you were to do a spiritual heart checkup, what would be revealed? What would Jesus your "spiritual doctor" recommend?

_____
_____
_____

What is your current appetite for the holiness of God? Have you lost it and want it back? Have you never had it but want to experience it for the first time? How can you tell?

_____
_____
_____

---

[4] Charles Wesley, "And Can It Be That I Should Gain?" from *Worship The Lord: Hymnal of the Church of God* (Anderson, IN: Warner Press, 1989), 234.

What I'm hearing God say to me

WEEK 2
Killing Sin before Sin Kills Us

Study Day 1

We lived in Texas for eighteen years. When we moved there, we were told how important it was to have your house treated regularly for pests. We took that advice to heart and treated our home because we wanted to live in it, and we wanted to make sure all the bugs didn't. No matter what we did, however, some still slipped in. That was especially true in the heat of the summer after a long stretch of rain. Somehow, no matter what we did, a few roaches crept in. Big tree roaches. I was usually made aware of their presence when one of my daughters began to scream—or refused to re-enter her room—until the vile creature was eradicated.

Roach eradication requires more than just a good effort, though. That roach actually had to die. Truthfully, in order to satisfy my kids, it usually required proof of death. There needed to be a body, a dead and lifeless body, for them to finally believe that the frightful invader was no more.

Now, bear in mind that my house had been well-treated for bugs. It was largely pest free, but some still got in. When that happened, I didn't award them for their craftiness, bravery, and well-honed survival skills. I didn't make a bed for them to sleep in. I didn't give them a place to eat at the table. They did not become our newest pets. We didn't think they were cute and put up with them or hope they would get what they wanted and be on their way. *We killed them*. We did it as fast as we could and by any means necessary.

In order to pursue a life of holiness before God, we must do the same with sin. Many years ago, Puritan pastor John Owen wrote, "Be killing sin or it will be killing you."[1] Sin is our enemy. It is the enemy of holiness and holy living. It seeks to kill any and all signs and influence of Jesus in our lives. That's why we have to fight to kill sin before it kills us.

So what is sin, anyway? A small word, *sin*, packs a big punch. It literally means "missing the mark." What mark? It is the mark of God's holy standard. Because God is the sovereign Creator of the heavens and the earth, "sustaining all things by his powerful word" (Hebrews 1:3), he determines right from wrong. In short, he sets the mark.

With that in mind, the Bible describes sin in many ways. First John 5:17 says, "All wrongdoing is sin." Sin includes every bad thing we have ever said, thought, or done. This is not a surprise. We expect sin to include all the bad stuff: murder, theft, slander, gossip, drunkenness, greed, etc. But that's not all. James 4:17 tells us, "If anyone…knows the good they ought to do and doesn't do it, it is sin for them." So sin includes all the good stuff that we fail to say, think, or do, as well. Good stuff

---
1 John Owen, *The Mortification of Sin* (Indianapolis: Urbanophile, LLC, 2019), Kindle location 151.

includes things such as listening to a friend instead of insisting on speaking myself, helping someone in need, sharing my resources with the poor, and serving my wife by doing the dishes even when I don't have to.

Now the list is growing much larger, isn't it? To add to it, sin must even include all the good things we actually do, but we do them for all the wrong reasons. That is the kind of thing Jesus was getting at in the Sermon on the Mount when he said, "Be careful not to practice your righteousness in front of others to be seen by them" (Matthew 6:1). Jesus also said we are to give and pray in secret so that we don't draw attention to ourselves.[2] We could go on to include any good deed done for selfish reasons. With all of this, the list is enormous.

When Paul was building his case that both Jews and Gentiles were alike when it came to sin, he left no doubt about how big the problem actually was. Here is how he put it in Romans 3:10–18:

> "There is no one righteous, not even one;
>   there is no one who understands;
>   there is no one who seeks God.
> All have turned away,
>   they have together become worthless;
> there is no one who does good,
>   not even one."
> "Their throats are open graves;
>   their tongues practice deceit."
> "The poison of vipers is on their lips."
>   "Their mouths are full of cursing and bitterness."
> "Their feet are swift to shed blood;
>   ruin and misery mark their ways,
> and the way of peace they do not know."
>   "There is no fear of God before their eyes."

That's pretty damning stuff. No one reads it and feels encouraged or thinks that sin is no big deal or that it doesn't apply to them. And if that wasn't enough, Paul wrote in Ephesians 2:1, 3 that we were "dead in…transgressions and sins" and "by nature deserving of wrath." We are all sinners. We were born with Adam's spiritual DNA, meaning that we all have a sin nature.[3] We are not sinners because we sin. It is much worse than that—we sin because we are sinners.

We definitely have a problem. We need to be saved from this sin. We need a Savior.

---

2 See Matthew 6:2–15.
3 See Romans 5:12–21.

Do you see sin more like parking tickets that aren't that big of a deal unless you get too many of them, or like cancer cells in your body that cause spiritual sickness and death? Why?

_____
_____
_____

If you understand that sin is more than simply the bad stuff you say, think, or do, but also includes the good stuff you fail to do and even the good stuff you do for the wrong reasons, how does this give you an honest spiritual picture of yourself?

_____
_____
_____

What is the difference between someone who is sin-obsessed verses someone who is permissive about sin? What is the danger in each position? Which have you been more prone to in your life? Why?

_____
_____
_____

What I'm hearing God say to me

Study Day 2

One of the most well-known biblical case studies about sin is the story of adultery, conspiracy, and murder in the life of King David.[1] It begins with David seeing a beautiful woman named Bathsheba bathing. That was innocent and unintentional. No sin there. But he let his eye linger. He desired her. And the chain reaction of sin began. He inquired about her and heard she was married to one of his best soldiers, Uriah. That didn't stop him. He wanted her anyway, so he sent for her and slept with her.

David thought that would be the end, but it wasn't. Bathsheba got pregnant. He brought her husband home from the battlefield and tried to cover things up by getting him to sleep with his wife. David thought that would be the end, too, but it wasn't. Uriah refused to cooperate. He didn't think it would be right to go home and sleep with his wife when the other soldiers were in the field.

So David sent Uriah back to the fighting with a message to the commander to arrange for Uriah to be killed in battle. David thought that would be the end, too, but it wasn't. The Bible doesn't specifically say it, but people had to know at least some elements of this sordid tale. No king can do all that without people knowing. No cover-up works that well. But even more significant than people knowing, *God* knew David's sin.

David's sin is a metaphor for our own sin patterns. He wrote about his journey from sin and shame to repentance in Psalms 32 and 51. Obviously his sin affected other people, especially Uriah and the child, who both died as a result of his sin, but it wasn't limited to that. Sin always causes collateral damage. Sometimes we can see it, and sometimes we can't. In David's case, the violence done later to his daughter Tamar and the eventual breakdown of his relationship with his son Absalom likely had their seeds in David's sin many years before.[2]

David's sin hurt others, but it was also sin against God. In Psalm 51, traditionally considered to be David's confession of what he had done, he wrote, "I know my transgressions, and my sin is always before me. Against you, you only, have I sinned and done what is evil in your sight" (verses 3–4). In Psalm 32, David described the weight of his sin as being so strong he could actually sense it physically: "When I kept silent, my bones wasted away through my groaning all day long. For day and night your hand was heavy upon me; my strength was sapped as in the heat of summer" (verses 3–4).

---

1 See 2 Samuel 11—12.
2 See 2 Samuel 13—19.

Sinning against others is real and heavy, but it doesn't compare to the offense against a holy God. Sin built a wall or created a chasm between David and God. Every sin does that. David was blind to sin's consequences. Because he was a religious man, it's safe to presume that he continued on with his daily prayers. He continued to obey God's Law (ignoring the adultery, lying, and murder parts, of course). He continued to sacrifice in the tabernacle as he was supposed to. I imagine that he continued speaking of being faithful to God and making sure to keep Israel faithful, too. I bet David continued to go through those motions, in complete and utter blindness, until he was exposed by God through the confrontation of the prophet Nathan.

Someone once said, "Sin will always take you farther than you wanted to go, keep you longer than you wanted to stay, and cost you more than you wanted to pay." That's so true! Even if we are conscious of the sin we are about to commit, we might tell ourselves that we'll only go so far. We just want to experiment a little, but then we find ourselves deep into it before we know it. We tell ourselves that we'll only dabble in sin for a short time. We just want to hang out for a little while, but then we find that we have become trapped and are unable to leave. We tell ourselves that it will only cost us a little. The price will be so small that we won't even miss it, but then we find that it costs us relationships, our reputation, and so much more. That's how sin works. David's story makes the point perfectly.

Think about the chain reaction of sin in David's life, how one thing led to another. When has a triggering event led to a chain reaction of sin in your life?

_____
_____
_____

Consider how David likely continued to go through the motions of worship, prayer, and sacrifice for a season until he was confronted by Nathan. How have you continued to go through the spiritual motions while remaining blind to sin in your own life?

_____
_____
_____

How do you react to the idea of sin taking you farther than you wanted to go, keeping you longer than you wanted to stay, and costing you more than you wanted to pay? How has that been true in your own life?

What I'm hearing God say to me

Study Day 3

Obviously, David didn't wake up one morning and decide to blow up his life. He wasn't looking to commit adultery, conspiracy, and murder. So how did it happen? The short answer is that David's sin was rooted in something else below the surface, a sin beneath the sin. That's what caused the chain reaction of sin in David's life.

Our sinfulness is not simply related to isolated acts. It is deep within our nature as fallen human beings, tied to the original sin of Adam and Eve back in the garden of Eden. Just like them, we sin because of a drive in our hearts, whether we are conscious of it or not. It's a sin underneath our sins. Martin Luther explained it this way: "The sin underneath all our sins is to trust the lie of the serpent that we cannot trust the love and grace of Christ and must take matters into our own hands."[1] That is why we chase power, wealth, pleasure, fame, acceptance from others, etc. as a substitute for satisfaction and contentment in the holiness of God.

In our sin, we "suppress the truth" (Romans 1:18). Even though God has revealed himself to us, we "neither glorified him as God nor gave thanks to him" (Romans 1:21). This has made us futile in our thinking and darkened our hearts. Ultimately, we "exchanged the truth about God for a lie, and worshiped and served created things rather than the Creator" (Romans 1:25). We "were made to (1) worship and serve God, and then (2) to rule over all created things in God's name," but instead, our sin caused us "to (1) worship and serve created things, and therefore (2) the created things came to rule over" us.[2] What we did in our sin was turn to an idol, a competing love that replaced God as our ultimate love. Though the text doesn't specifically say it, that is what David did. It's what we all do in one form or another.

When we talk about idols, we tend to think of ancient statues that Indiana Jones went searching for in dusty temples. We think we are smarter and more sophisticated than those primitive and superstitious people from centuries ago because we know that statues aren't real gods.

True, we don't worship statues. But we do worship idols.

In the ancient world, idols were everywhere, and they weren't just statues then. They represented something people couldn't live without or a power they desperately wanted or needed. They were worshiped in order to receive some benefit or to prevent some loss. Fertility, prosperity, pleasure, power, etc. all had expressions in one of many different idols. Back then, devotion was measured by the value of the sacrifice, the quality of the shrine, or the time and energy spent in worship.

---

1 Martin Luther, "Martin Luther > Quotes > Quotable Quote," from *Goodreads*, accessed November 13, 2019, https://www.goodreads.com/quotes/643934-the-sin-underneath-all-our-sins-is-to-trust-the.
2 Timothy Keller, *Gospel in Life* (Grand Rapids: Zondervan, 2010), 37.

Our world is filled with idols, and neither are they just statues today. They still represent something we can't live without or a power we desperately want or need: Wall Street says money, Washington says power, Harvard says intelligence, Hollywood says beauty and fame, music and the arts say self-expression. Idols are everywhere. Devotion is still measured by the value of the sacrifice (our bank accounts), the quality of the shrine (a stadium, a house, a car), or the time and energy spent in worship (our social media accounts and our calendars).

Augustine said, "Idolatry is worshipping anything that ought to be used, or using anything that is meant to be worshipped."[3] That is true, but let's get even more basic. As a competing love that replaces God as our ultimate love, idols can be anything and have been everything. An idol captures your heart and imagination more than God. You seek for it to give you the security, satisfaction, and peace only God can give.

Somewhere along the way, David's heart and mind were captured by an idol—or several of them. At the very least, we see that he bowed to the idols of power, pleasure, and pride. Maybe there were others as well. At the most basic level, David made something else his ultimate love instead of God. He worshiped it. He surrendered to it. He obeyed it. That is what led him to adultery, conspiracy, and murder.

The same is true for you and me. Our worship, surrender, and obedience to idols lead us further into sin all the time. Here are just three quick examples: We think life will only be worth living if we have a certain amount of money or the right house or car, so we make all kinds of decisions driven by greed and envy. Or we believe nothing is more important than having the approval of a certain person or group, so we do whatever it takes, including surrendering our integrity, tearing other people down, or even taking things that don't belong to us, to get it. Or we want to be loved by a certain person so much that we will sacrifice any friendship, ignore our family, or even offer up our body and our purity to have him or her. There's an idol behind every one of these sins, driving us to make them our ultimate love.

We have a problem. We need to be saved from our idols that lead us further into sin. That is why we need a Savior. And we are saved through the Savior, Jesus Christ.

Being right with God is a direct result of the work of Jesus on our behalf. The New Testament spells out this reality over and over again, but I want to stay with Paul's description of Jesus' work in his letter to the Ephesian church. Here's how he put it in Ephesians 2:4–9:

> Because of his great love for us, God, who is rich in mercy, made us alive with Christ even when we were dead in transgressions—it is by grace you have been saved. And God raised us up with Christ and seated us with him

---

[3] Attributed to Augustine of Hippo, from QuoteTab, accessed March 24, 2020, https://www.quotetab.com/quote/by-saint-augustine/idolatry-is-worshipping-anything-that-ought-to-be-used-or-using-anything-that-is?source=idolatry.

in the heavenly realms in Christ Jesus, in order that in the coming ages he might show the incomparable riches of his grace, expressed in his kindness to us in Christ Jesus. For it is by grace you have been saved, through faith—and this is not from yourselves, it is the gift of God—not by works, so that no one can boast.

Our salvation is Jesus' doing, from start to finish.

Salvation came through Jesus' sacrifice on the cross, where sin was defeated, and his resurrection, where death met its end. Ephesians 2:1–3 says that we were spiritually lifeless, hopeless, and under judgment. Still, God came to our rescue. God came to us, through Jesus, in mercy. We received God's kindness in place of the justice we deserved. He also came to us in grace, where we received his unmerited favor and generosity toward us. In love, we received God's self-sacrificing, self-giving action for us and toward us. Finally, in kindness, God's gentle action blessed us with himself in the present and, especially, in eternity.

God essentially acted in two ways: (1) Jesus died on the cross to pay the penalty for our sin and heal the breach our sinful brokenness created. He offers us this healing by grace, through faith. This makes us alive. Faith is our simple trust in who Jesus is and what he did to save us. It leads to a life that shows and declares God's glory. And (2) the Holy Spirit works in our hearts to awaken us spiritually to the truth of God. We see our sinful brokenness. We see what Jesus has done. We respond in faith and are saved, then we are made eternally joyful and alive for the first time.

We are saved by faith, not because we are prettier, smarter, more gifted, or more moral. We are not even saved because we have more faith than someone else. Faith is not a competition with others. It's not about passing a test. Faith is about putting your imperfect trust in a perfect Jesus. He is the one who saves. So everything, even our faith, is based on grace.

God says we are worth the life of his Son. That is not just for some people who might seem to deserve it or even for the "ideal" person you wish you could be—it includes you just as you are. Jesus died to make all of us alive. And God now sees us through the sacrifice of his Son. Through the power of Jesus, God makes us a trophy of his grace. He is saying, "Look at what I can do with your sinful brokenness!"

How much do you think sin is a series of isolated acts and how much of it is really driven by service to an idol beneath the surface, deep in your heart? Why do you say so?

_____
_____
_____

What idols have you been most tempted by in your life? How has that changed over the years? What idols are tempting you most today?

_____
_____
_____

What I'm hearing God say to me

_____
_____
_____
_____
_____
_____
_____
_____
_____
_____
_____
_____
_____
_____
_____
_____
_____
_____
_____
_____
_____

Study Day 4

The key to unlocking the door of faith is repentance. As we said before, *holiness is the work of God in us whereby Jesus takes full ownership of our lives, purifies us from sin, and sets us apart for his service.* We are made holy to be wholly his. But given the reality of sin, there needs to be a way to free us from sin's poison in order to be wholly his. And repentance is that way. It is the first step and a necessary ongoing step in pursuing a holy life. *Repentance is the Holy Spirit–produced sorrow over sin that leads to confession, contrition, and a direct change in the course of our lives from sin to God.* When repentance is real, it involves words, heart change, and action. It's both a gift and a fight. More on that in a bit.

Repentance is always present at the beginning of our life in Christ, but it doesn't stop there. Repentance is present throughout our life in Christ in more ways and at more times than we can ever count. Nearly every time we grow in Christ and are changed, it is preceded by some measure of repentance and deeper faith in him. In fact, the life of holiness always means a life of regular and conscientious repentance. As Packer suggests, "Growth in holiness cannot continue where repenting from the heart has stopped."[1]

Believe it or not, repentance is a gift.

Remember when you were a kid and you got a bad cough, maybe even bronchitis? After a while, it makes your throat so sore that it feels raw. It prevents you from doing all the normal things in your day. It even makes it hard to sleep at night. At some point, the doctor prescribes the dreaded medicine—cough syrup! There is a reason cough syrup hasn't been synthesized into a flavor for ice cream, candy, or snow cones. It's gross! That's why they camouflage the taste with grape or bubble-gum flavor so that you will swallow it. So we try to put off taking the medicine. We hope things will get better on their own. When they don't fix themselves, we try our own quick fixes. Cough syrup may be the cure, but we don't want to take it.

That's how Satan's first lie works in our lives. At first, Satan gets us to think that sin is no big deal. He may even try to get us to believe that if it gets serious enough, we can always repent later. So we sin, and the consequences are instantly damaging. More than that, the longer and deeper we go into sin, the worse it gets.

Then Satan springs the trap. He throws the second lie at us, trying to convince us that repentance is impossible. Here is how Puritan pastor Thomas Brooks put it: "He who now tempts you to sin upon this account, that repentance is easy, will, before long, to work you to despair, and forever to break the neck of your soul, present

---
1 Packer, 127.

repentance as the most difficult and hardest work in the world."[2] At first, we don't think we need the medicine. We don't need to choke down that nasty cough syrup. Then, things are so bad that we don't think the medicine will work. We are too far gone and think we can't "make things right with God."

But repentance is not like cough syrup, and we are never so far gone that we can't make things right with God.

Imagine you are walking around in a heavily insulated parka. I'm talking about the kind that is rated to keep you nice and warm in arctic winters. Now, imagine you are wearing that parka on the hottest day of the year in the middle of the Sahara desert—you know, when it's just a mild 120 degrees outside. You would be literally dying from the heat. That's what carrying sin around is like. It separates us from God and others, and it kills us spiritually. Remember Satan's two lies about repentance? You will soon be dead whether you know it or not. You need to be set free, and fast.

Repentance is the zipper on that parka. It's a gift that frees us from the spiritual consequences of sin and makes us right with God. There is never a time that we are too far gone and never a time when God will ignore or reject a repentant heart that turns to him.

Repentance is the pathway for being saved *from* our sin *through* Jesus Christ. When you understand the gift of repentance, you also see how much you need it to be a regular part of your life with God. You never outgrow your need for it.

As you grow in Christ, there is a constant awareness of two things: (1) *How far you have come in being made new*. Remember the "awed adoration" we discussed in Week 1? This should produce praise and thanksgiving to God for the wonderful gift of his holiness, which is alive in you. And (2) *How far you still have to go*. This should produce a deep humility and an appreciation for the mercy and grace of God. The gift of repentance is what made and continues to make this possible.

Have you typically thought of repentance as a gift or a burden? Has that view served you well? Why or why not?

_____
_____

If repentance is the pathway to getting back to and staying right with God, why do we avoid it so much?

_____
_____

---

[2] Thomas Brooks, *Precious Remedies Against Satan's Devices* (Philadelphia: Jonathan Pounder, 1810), 40.

How have you fallen victim to Satan's lies about repentance: (1) Your sin isn't a big deal and (2) When you do see how bad your sin is, repentance isn't possible?

_____
_____
_____

What I'm hearing God say to me

_____
_____
_____
_____
_____
_____
_____
_____
_____
_____
_____
_____
_____
_____
_____
_____
_____
_____
_____
_____
_____
_____
_____

Study Day 5

Our thanksgiving and deep humility should generate a conviction to fight the fight that kills sin before it kills us. And make no mistake, it's a fight. Rejecting the old idols that have come to define our passions and desires and replacing them with the things of God is a fight. Not growing complacent or weary along the way is a fight. Declaring to ourselves over and over again that we are right with God because of what Jesus has done and not what we do is a fight. Walking a new path away from sin and toward God is a fight. Pursuing a holy life requires that fight.

Because sin is out to kill us, we need to kill it first. That is why we should never give sin a place to live in our lives. And, if it finds a way in, we need to get it out as soon as possible. We don't compromise with it, excuse it, or ignore it. We don't give it even a little space. We need to kill sin before it kills us. It's always a fight, but it's a fight we must win.

That is why repentance is not only a gift, but it's also our chief weapon in the fight to kill sin before it kills us. When we repent, not only are we purging ourselves of the poison of sin that is destroying us, but we are also declaring that God is our ultimate satisfaction and joy. We want God and his holiness more than we want sin in our lives.

Here is how we fight with sin and win.

J. C. Ryle wrote that "the first step towards attaining a higher standard of holiness is to realize more fully the amazing sinfulness of sin."[1] First, by the power of the Holy Spirit, we are convicted of our sin. As Jesus said, the Holy Spirit "will prove the world to be in the wrong about sin and righteousness and judgment" (John 16:8). Being convicted means knowing how wrong sin is and understanding the poison it has spread. That's why our fight has to begin here. Perhaps one of the reasons sin gains such influence in our lives is that we sometimes forget just how ugly and destructive it is. We see "everybody else doing it" and then don't see a problem for us. Other times, we honestly just want what sin brings more than we want what God gives us. Either way, conviction involves a fight just to see sin as sin.

The next step is confession. Confession means taking responsibility for our actions and telling the truth about who we are and what we have done. The fight here is between telling the truth, and the whole truth, versus being general or generic. Because we don't want to admit that we have done anything wrong or that we can't fix whatever is broken, we would much rather say "I'm not perfect" or "I have issues." But that's not confession; it's image management. Instead, true confession says, "I lied when I said that." "I envied that car." "I lusted after that girl." We win the fight by being honest and transparent in every respect, as much as we are able.

---
1 Ryle, 20.

Confession has two dimensions: a vertical one (between us and God) and a horizontal one (between us and others). Regarding the vertical dimension, 1 John 1:9 says, "If we confess our sins, he is faithful and just and will forgive us our sins and purify us from all unrighteousness." There is no repentance without the vertical dimension being addressed because, ultimately, all sin is directly against God; therefore, he deserves to hear the truth about our sin. It's not a mystery to him. We are not giving him new information. That's not what confession is for. Confession's purpose is to offer an open and pliable heart to God. Its goal is the restoration of a right relationship with a holy God.

The horizontal dimension is important, too. James 5:16 advises us, "Confess your sins to each other and pray for each other so that you may be healed." This dimension is equally dependent on truth-telling and transparency. What's critical here is that we want to do whatever is in our power to right the broken relationship that exists between us and others. Being willing to take this "horizontal" step says a lot about the true state of our heart in the vertical dimension. In other words, if we are unwilling to do our part in the horizontal realm, we are effectively saying that we are unwilling to fully obey and honor God in the vertical realm.

Following right behind confession is the fight of contrition. When we win this fight, we will feel bad—horrible even—about our sin. This feeling is not just the result of getting caught or feeling embarrassed. That's just regret. Instead, it's a deep sorrow of the heart, a "godly sorrow," as Paul described it in 2 Corinthians 7:10. Feeling bad about our sin, realizing just how hot we are in the parka in the Sahara Desert, changes our hearts. It breaks down our pride and self-sufficiency and drives us to seek God's forgiveness.

On the one hand, we have to fight our tendency to act superior, as though we don't need forgiveness. On the other hand, we have to fight against our tendency to act inferior, as though forgiveness for us isn't even possible. The fight is won when we freely admit who we are (sinners in need of forgiveness) and who God is (a merciful and gracious God who longs to forgive us). This causes us to quickly ask for forgiveness because we know we need God's mercy and grace.

We ask for mercy because we don't want to receive the punishment we deserve for our sin. We ask for grace because we want to receive the gift of God's unmerited favor and love that we don't deserve. When we ask this from God, we trust in faith that we will receive it because God is "faithful and just" and will "purify us from all unrighteousness" (1 John 1:9). It's also why we "pray for each other" (James 5:16) in the midst of our mutual confession. Again, we are calling on God's power to be brought to bear upon our relational brokenness so that we might be further cleansed by the mercy and grace we offer to one another. This assurance of forgiveness opens the "zipper on the parka." It is the experience of deliverance from sin's power.

With the peace that comes through forgiveness, there is a change in our hearts. This change in our hearts produces a change in our walk with God and with others. There is a new direction in our lives toward holiness and away from sin. That new direction is one that honors God with new thoughts, words, and actions that are in line with his will and way.

As John the Baptist admonished the crowds, we, too, are to "produce fruit in keeping with repentance" (Matthew 3:8). The fight is with sin's inertia, which constantly pulls us to remain in the same patterns as before. Sometimes we might even bask in the false comfort that we have talked repentance, verbalizing words of confession and pleas for forgiveness even though we have not actually produced any fruit. We have to fight against this all the time. The fight is won, however, when we replace the old patterns of sin with new patterns that are in line with God's righteousness and holiness. Those new patterns are the fruit of new, Holy Spirit–driven desires to want the holiness of God over our sin. They always produce a turning, even a dramatic turning, from one direction to another.

The details will vary. There are times when our hearts want those new patterns and that leads us to obey. There are other times when we obey despite the fact that our hearts don't yet want what God wants. We obey because he commands us to do so and we want to please him. We trust that God will change our hearts in time. Either way, obedience will guide us in the overall holy and God-pleasing direction of a changed life.

Though there are seasons when the fight with sin is more intense than in others, the fight never ends on this side of heaven. It's a fight that we must fight, and it's a fight that we must win. To do so, we need to mobilize all the spiritual resources at our disposal, from the whole armor of God to the community and support of God's people.[2] Remember what Paul said about us: "We are God's handiwork, created in Christ Jesus to do good works, which God prepared in advance for us to do" (Ephesians 2:10). Repentance is the pathway for being saved *from* our sin *through* Jesus Christ. The result of repentance is a life lived *for* being God's workmanship. That means being the kind of people who love holiness, who love what God loves, and who want to be God's man or woman above anything else. Repentance is the gift that makes it all possible. It is our chief weapon in the fight to kill sin before sin kills us.

---

2 See Ephesians 6:10–20 and Hebrews 10:24–25.

What is the difference between regret and repentance? How do you know when you are seeing real repentance?

_____
_____
_____

Two key verses on repentance are 1 Jonn 1:9 (the vertical dimension) and James 5:16 (the horizontal dimension). Why is the vertical aspect of repentance important? Why is the horizontal aspect of repentance important? What does each accomplish?

_____
_____
_____

Where are you in the fight against sin—advancing, on guard, retreating, defeated, surrendered? Why do you say so?

_____
_____
_____

What I'm hearing God say to me

WEEK 3
A Life in the Yes Position

Study Day 1

My youngest daughter, Katelyn, was a cheerleader in the eighth grade, a flyer, specifically. She learned a bunch of cheers, had an outfit for every occasion, and was excited and ready, filled with energy. Her squad cheered for the football and basketball teams. They had performances during time outs, between quarters, and at every significant part of the game. They cheered when the game was on the line and when it wasn't. They cheered whether the team was up or down. And while it was, of course, more fun when the team won, the cheerleaders were out in full force regardless—even when their team was getting killed.

Nothing stopped them from cheering their team on to victory. That's expected. That's how it should be, everyone eagerly cheering for their favorite team to win. They do so despite the odds that might be stacked against them (think Chicago Cubs or Cleveland Browns). When their team wins, they cheer the loudest. When their team loses, they are the first ones to encourage them with "There's always next game" or "There's always next year." That's what cheerleaders do.

We could all use a few cheerleaders in our lives, especially as we pursue a life of holiness. When our hearts aren't really motivated to please God or when we have no desire to know him deeply (Week 1), we need cheerleaders to pump us up. When the fight to kill sin before it kills us has us feeling defeated (Week 2), we need cheerleaders to encourage us to get up and get back into the fight. When everything in us wants to say *no* to God's voice because what he is asking us to do seems too hard or too costly, we need cheerleaders to encourage us to say *yes*.

Make no mistake, though. As theologian Kevin DeYoung says, "The world provides no cheerleaders on the pathway to godliness."[1] The world we live in is largely ignorant of what godliness is, and when it does have a clue about it, it is largely resistant to the whole idea. We should expect that kind of response from people far from God. However, such an attitude can even be found in people who claim to be Christian.

To be clear, the life *whereby Jesus takes full ownership of our lives, purifies us from sin, and sets us apart for his service* will not receive acclaim and praise from the wider world around us. That has been true in every culture throughout history. And yet, God is still calling us to be holy to be wholly his—and the Holy Spirit is still working on our behalf—and scores of God's people are still saying *yes*, even when the wider world around them isn't cheering them on.

Those who say *yes* to God desire a right relationship with him. There are many places where that is laid out in the Scriptures, but an important one involves a parable Jesus told, as recorded in Matthew 25:1–13:

---
1 DeYoung, Kindle location 531.

"At that time the kingdom of heaven will be like ten virgins who took their lamps and went out to meet the bridegroom. Five of them were foolish and five were wise. The foolish ones took their lamps but did not take any oil with them. The wise ones, however, took oil in jars along with their lamps. The bridegroom was a long time in coming, and they all became drowsy and fell asleep.

"At midnight the cry rang out: 'Here's the bridegroom! Come out to meet him!'

"Then all the virgins woke up and trimmed their lamps. The foolish ones said to the wise, 'Give us some of your oil; our lamps are going out.'

" 'No,' they replied, 'there may not be enough for both us and you. Instead, go to those who sell oil and buy some for yourselves.'

"But while they were on their way to buy the oil, the bridegroom arrived. The virgins who were ready went in with him to the wedding banquet. And the door was shut.

"Later the others also came. 'Lord, Lord,' they said, 'open the door for us!'

"But he replied, 'Truly I tell you, I don't know you.'

"Therefore keep watch, because you do not know the day or the hour."

Every one of the virgins in the story represents a prospective disciple of Jesus. Some are foolish and some are wise, but you cannot tell based on their initial appearance. They are all waiting for the bridegroom to come. That bridegroom is the Messiah, the deliverer sent from God for whom the Jewish people had been waiting for generations. One day, that Messiah would come and gather all the faithful people of God. Now, because you didn't know when the Messiah would come, you needed to be prepared. Wise preparation meant that you were sure you had enough oil to keep your lamp lit. That would determine whether you were wise or foolish.

Jesus clearly was the Messiah. That was true based upon everything that was said about him through the prophets, and it was true, even more importantly, based on everything he did and everything he said about himself. So, what does the oil signify? It's what really counts in the end. Oil is the evidence of a transformed life, the fruit of Jesus taking full ownership of a person's life. Examples of that would be evident in the heart and actions of each disciple (see, for example, the Parable of the Sheep and the Goats in Matthew 25:31–46).

Time is very important here, as with many of Jesus' parables. The virgins/prospective disciples didn't know when the bridegroom/Messiah would appear. No one thought he would come at midnight, so everyone was asleep. No worries; that would be expected. However, being able to sleep does not necessarily mean being ready. The foolish ones didn't expect the bridegroom/Messiah to come when he did, so they weren't prepared, and when he came, there was nothing they could do. The wise ones didn't expect the bridegroom/Messiah to come then either, but they were ready. Their lives were prepared. They had oil.

Only the ones with oil could trim their lamps. They were the wise ones, and they would be ready to meet the bridegroom/Messiah. Only they would get admitted to the wedding banquet. The wedding banquet represents the time of eternal salvation and rest in heaven brought about when the Messiah returns. It is open to all, but to be admitted you have to be ready when the bridegroom comes. You have to have oil.

The other virgins wanted to be admitted to the banquet, too. No one wants to be left out of this celebration, even those who refused to prepare for it when they had the chance. But now the doors are locked. Now the moment is passed, and the bridegroom doesn't know them. It's too late.

Jesus closed with the punchline, "Therefore keep watch, because you do not know the day or the hour" (verse 13). To keep watch literally means to be prepared. The emphasis is on knowing the bridegroom, which means you will be consistent in your discipleship and confident in Jesus' promise to return. Anyone can be a peacemaker for a night, merciful for a day, or compassionate to some, but that is not the same thing as knowing the bridegroom. That is why we have to "be prepared." Right relationship with Jesus is everything.

Having a right relationship with Jesus is not simply praying a prayer and stating belief in a set of doctrines. That's not even remotely scriptural. Right relationship fundamentally means we know God through Jesus Christ. Paul put it like this in Titus 3:3–7:

> At one time we too were foolish, disobedient, deceived and enslaved by all kinds of passions and pleasures. We lived in malice and envy, being hated and hating one another. But when the kindness and love of God our Savior appeared, he saved us, not because of righteous things we had done, but because of his mercy. He saved us through the washing of rebirth and renewal by the Holy Spirit, whom he poured out on us generously through Jesus Christ our Savior, so that, having been justified by his grace, we might become heirs having the hope of eternal life.

Remember, we are saved *from* our sin *through* Jesus Christ.

Who have been the cheerleaders in your life that have encouraged you to know Jesus or to grow in him? Whom have *you* been a cheerleader for?

_____

_____

_____

How can a godly cheerleader help when your heart isn't motivated to know God deeply or please him? How can a cheerleader help us say *yes* to God when we want to say *no*?

Thinking about Jesus' Parable of the Ten Virgins, how are you making sure there is oil in your lamp? What does it mean for you to be prepared for the coming bridegroom?

What I'm hearing God say to me

Study Day 2

Before we received the saving gift of Jesus by grace through faith, we did not and could not have right relationship with God. Our sin made sure of that. Because of our sin, we couldn't fix this relationship. We couldn't make any oil. We couldn't be ready. We couldn't know God.

Jesus fixed it for us. He was perfectly holy and righteous. He graciously took the penalty for our sin on himself when he died on the cross. That is what it means that "the kindness and love of God our Savior appeared" (Titus 3:4). At that moment, in love, Jesus made salvation possible for all who would receive him, and he produced the oil. God knows us and relates to us as his very own now because of "the washing of rebirth and renewal by the Holy Spirit, whom he poured out on us generously through Jesus Christ our Savior" (Titus 3:5–6). Now we are "heirs having the hope of eternal life" (Titus 3:7).

Remember, those of us who have received salvation through Jesus now live *for* being God's workmanship. That life is a direct result of a life of repentance. We don't need to rehash all of Week 2 again, but it is important to understand clearly what repentance means at the moment one receives the oil of salvation in Jesus. It's vitally important to know that there is no grace without the true repentance that comes from a guilty plea about our sin.

A few years ago, I was in a hurry on my way to work one day. I was approaching an intersection when the light turned yellow. I should have stopped, but in my haste I hit the gas and drove through. It was red before I entered the intersection—and there was a waiting police officer who saw it all. He simply motioned to me to make a quick left and pull over. Once I did that, I saw a number of other police officers with many other people who were pulled over just like me. That was a busy intersection and one that many people had been speeding through, so the police had set up a little sting operation for folks such as me.

You know what happened next: I got a ticket. No shock there. However, when I read over the ticket I noticed something at the bottom. I had different legal options before me, three in fact. I could plead innocent, no contest, or guilty. Innocent meant I didn't run the red light. I couldn't really make that claim even though I wished I could. Guilty meant I did it and I took responsibility for it, which I just didn't want to do. No contest sounded better. That meant I admitted I wasn't perfect, so there was a chance that I did something wrong. I wouldn't contest that. However, it didn't come with the label of "guilty" and I could still feel innocent.

That is often our attitude toward sin.

We want to plead innocent and blame someone else or some circumstance that is out of our hands. But here is the thing: we cannot plead innocent and receive grace. In fact, pleading innocent means we don't need grace. As crazy as that seems, we are effectively saying we have no sin that needs forgiveness.

If pleading innocent doesn't work, then we want to go for no contest. We won't dispute the reality of sin, but we won't admit it, either. We definitely don't want to admit the depth and breadth of it. The best we will do is say "I'm not perfect" or "I know I have issues" or "I'm just like everyone else." Just as with a plea of innocence, pleading no contest also means that we don't really need grace because we aren't really sinners.

When it comes to sin, only a guilty plea works. A guilty plea is a frank and candid admission of our sin before a holy God. It's not leaving anything out or being generic. It's completely owning up to the truth of who we are and what we have done. Author C. S. Lewis argued, "A man who admits no guilt can accept no forgiveness."[1] Grace is experienced only after an admission of guilt and an expression of need. We confess our sin before a holy God, whose ways are not our ways, and we place our trust in a God who is love, whose love for us is so full that his Son willingly sacrificed his life for us. When we plead guilty, we receive Jesus' grace and the total and absolute forgiveness of our sin. We confess our sin, repent, and ask for God's forgiveness. Through that path of repentance, we enter into right relationship with God through Jesus. It's the only way.

When we have a right relationship with God through Jesus, he grants us the oil we need to be ready when the bridegroom comes. Not only that, but also, because we know him, we are now wise unto salvation and no longer foolish. By the power of the Holy Spirit and the grace of Jesus, we accumulate more and more oil. We become receptors and distributors of the love and glory of God because we are made holy and pursue a holy life in Jesus. That is what it means to live *for* being God's workmanship.

How is it that we can accept the idea of sin, or even that we are sinners, but have such a hard time actually pleading guilty to actual sin in our lives? In what ways do you struggle with this?

_____

_____

_____

---

[1] C. S. Lewis, *The Problem of Pain* (New York: HarperCollins, 1940), 125.

**C. S. Lewis wrote, "A man who admits no guilt can accept no forgiveness."
What sins do you find it difficult to admit?**

What I'm hearing God say to me

week 3 day 2

Study Day 3

Right relationship naturally—or rather, supernaturally—produces right posture.

This right posture is a key sign that you have the oil of salvation and are ready for the bridegroom to come. But if we are not careful, we can become what theologian Dallas Willard called "a 'vampire Christian.' One in effect says to Jesus: 'I'd like a little of your blood, please. But I don't care to be your student or have your character. In fact, won't you just excuse me while I get on with my life, and I'll see you in heaven.' "[1] People who have this kind of posture are the ones in this story whom Jesus said he doesn't know. They are the foolish virgins who don't have enough oil when the bridegroom comes. They are not ready, and so are shut out of the wedding feast.

So if this posture is wrong, what is the right posture?

Right posture means right stance. Think of a runner in the starting block, a catcher behind the plate, a marksman at the firing range, a violinist in position. Stance matters if you are going to play your position well. A person in right relationship with God through Jesus Christ stands in the *yes* position.[2]

Remember, we are now "hidden with Christ in God" (Colossians 3:3) which is a gift, but we also must "put to death" (Colossians 3:5) whatever remains of our old identity apart from Christ and "put on" (Colossians 3:10) whatever reflects the character and countenance of Jesus, which is a daily fight (Week 1). We have the spiritual DNA of Jesus through our new birth in him by grace and through faith, but we need to realize this new life in practice. As pastor John Piper explains, "If a child is to grow into the fullest expression of his Father's character, he needs both the DNA by virtue of birth and the practice of that character with the help of his father's discipline. In other words, we need regeneration by God's seed, and we need sanctification by God's Spirit—in order to grow up into the full participation in his holiness."[3] That is what the *yes* position is all about.

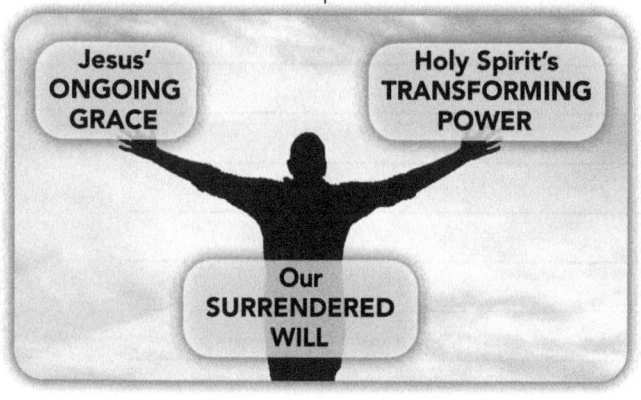

The *yes* position is a simultaneous merger of Jesus' ongoing grace, the Holy Spirit's power, and our surrendered will. It is for every area of our lives. That's what Paul meant when he

---

1 Dallas Willard, "Why Bother With Discipleship?" from Dallas Willard Ministries, accessed March 6, 2025, https://dwillard.org/resources/articles/why-bother-with-discipleship.
2 This is a concept I first heard from my late mentor and friend, Gil Stafford. I don't remember the origin. I have adapted it some, but the idea is his.
3 John Piper, "Prelude to Acting the Miracle," in *Acting the Miracle*, ed. John Piper and David Mathis (Wheaton, IL: Crossway, 2013), 31.

prayed, "May God himself, the God of peace, sanctify you through and through. May your whole spirit, soul and body be kept blameless at the coming of our Lord Jesus Christ" (1 Thessalonians 5:23). *Sanctify* is such a weighty word. It means to consecrate something or to make it holy. As God does the work in us *whereby Jesus takes full ownership of our lives and works to make us perfect receptors and distributors of the love and glory of God*, we take up this right posture.

There is never a time when we are not in desperate need of Jesus' ongoing grace. We don't just need grace in order to get saved; we need grace to *stay* saved. We don't just need grace to begin life in Christ; we need grace to take every step along the way. Theologian Diane Leclerc says, "The way we can be holy is that God makes us holy as we cooperate with his grace. This is sanctification—God forming us spiritually into the likeness of Jesus Christ."[4] The grace of Jesus does that sanctifying work. Jesus' ongoing grace doesn't just keep us right with God, but it also causes his graciousness to exude from every area of our lives.

There is never a time when we are not in desperate need of the Holy Spirit's transforming power. In one sense, the Holy Spirit's power is like fuel for a car. Cars can't move without fuel. In another sense, the Holy Spirit's power is like new glasses that help us to see the world correctly for the first time. At best everything was blurry before, but now we can see everything as God wants us to. The Holy Spirit will not only empower us to do the hard work of obedience, but he also will challenge us to see areas of our lives that need to be changed more and more.

There is never a time when a holy life doesn't require our surrendered will. Obedience is more than a one-time declaration. It requires regular, daily, or even hourly surrender in ways big and small. It is an absolute commitment to obey Jesus and live by his teachings and example. It means living to do the things Jesus would do and say the things Jesus would say if he were physically walking in our shoes.

In what ways and areas do you need to receive Jesus' ongoing grace to continue the journey of saying yes to God?

_____
_____

In what ways and areas do you need the Holy Spirit's power to help you overcome a supernatural obstacle in your path toward saying yes?

_____
_____

---

4 Diane Leclerc, "Holiness and Sanctification as a Wesleyan Paradigm for Spiritual Formation," in *Spiritual Formation: A Wesleyan Paradigm*, eds. Diane Leclerc and Mark Maddix (Kansas City: Beacon Press, 2011), 49.

In what ways and areas do you need to surrender your will and obey God even if it's hard and even if you don't feel like it?

What I'm hearing God say to me

Study Day 4

In the *yes* position, our will and desire is to become like Christ. As Leclerc continues, "The Christian life, sustained by grace and the indwelling Holy Spirit, is a life of power, even a life of power over sin.... Nothing will ever take away our *ability* to sin. But the sanctified, Spirit-filled life does effectively deal with our 'propensity' to sin. The power of God is indeed greater than the power of sin, in the here and now."[1] We know that apart from the grace of Jesus to save us and the power of the Holy Spirit to transform us, we have no hope of right relationship with God. We also know that, apart from the grace of Jesus to save us and the power of the Holy Spirit to transform us, we have no ability to be in right posture before God. So, in the *yes* position, we always stand open with all of our will, as imperfect as it is, to the ongoing grace of Jesus and the power of the Holy Spirit.

As we said before, right relationship naturally, or rather supernaturally, produces right posture. You can see the *yes* position in action. Here are just a few examples.

By the time a marriage is in trouble, there is a long list of wounds on both sides. Words and actions cut deep. Emotional or physical neglect makes a heart cold. But what if a life in the *yes* position produced true repentance and forgiveness? I don't mean words with no actions to back them up. I certainly don't mean words spoken and forgotten soon after. I mean real and deep heartbreak over how hurts were caused, replacing pride and selfishness, causing repentance and a desire to change. Real compassion would replace a desire to hold grudges, and that would make forgiveness possible. The power to repent and forgive comes from Jesus. If he has power over sin and death, he has power over our marriages, too.

We know that racism is often bred by all kinds of false assumptions and mixed-up beliefs about others. People are raised on hate, and their victims are encouraged to nourish fear and a desire for revenge, too. The cycle of mistrust and hatred is pervasive. But what if a life in the *yes* position produced true "love your neighbor as yourself" kind of love from Jesus? I don't mean denying the reality of injustice, and I certainly don't mean politically correct platitudes or virtue signaling. I mean the supernatural creation of a new heart. I mean a deep desire to see people as Jesus sees them. I mean a love that transcends human possibilities. The power to love like that comes from Jesus. If he has power over sin and death, he has power over our hearts, too.

Sexual sin takes on many forms, from pornography to adultery and everything in between. Sexuality as a gift from God has been blurred by lust and covetousness in more ways than we can count. But what if a life in the *yes* position produced a pure

---
1 Leclerc., 52–53.

heart, one where we looked out for the interests of others and glorified God with our bodies?[2] The power for purity comes from Jesus. If he has power over sin and death, he has power over our polluted desires, too.

We live in a culture with an ever-increasing sense of need. Many of us are so consumed with getting more that we spend 110% of what we make. We crave the newest, brightest, and biggest thing out there—especially if we can have it before our friends do. We shop when we're happy, sad, or even bored. We never feel satisfied. But what if a life in the *yes* position produced a desire in us to find our lives by losing them in Christ?[3] What if we found our treasure in heaven and not on earth?[4] What if we were open-handed and ready to share?[5] The power to be generous comes from Jesus. If he has power over sin and death, he has power over our wallets, too.

We could go on. Examples of a transformed life in the *yes* position are limitless. Remember Paul's prayer for the Thessalonian church? He asked God to completely sanctify them, including body and soul and spirit—every part of their existence. That is what it means for Jesus to take full ownership of our lives. In that process, elements of our old lives before Christ, marked with sin, are removed and replaced with the new fruit of life in Christ, marked with his holiness and righteousness.

When we moved to Texas years ago, we lived first with a gracious family from our church and then in a small apartment for a few weeks. We eventually found a house and waited through all the inspection and closing time, eager to finally move into our new place. Finally, the day came. The moving truck rolled up to our new house and we piled out, with a great crew of volunteers right behind us.

We expected an empty house. We hoped it wouldn't be too messy. We wanted to quickly clean it and unload all of our stuff before we set out to paint and decorate the house to truly make it our own. What we got was nothing like that.

The previous owner hadn't moved out yet. All his stuff was still in the house. Not just some of it—all of it. And the owner wasn't even there. He was in Michigan and just had a few friends to meet us. As you can imagine, things were pretty tense at first.

The problem was that we owned the house, but only in theory. Our names were on all the legal papers, but the old owner still occupied the house. We had to move *his* stuff out in order to move *our* stuff in. After that, we had to clean, and only then could we decorate and make the house *our* house. It took a long time.

A house you don't own is not your house. A house you can't live in is not your house. A house that you can only partially live in is not your house, either. If a house

---

2 See 1 Corinthians 6:20.
3 See Matthew 10:39.
4 See Matthew 6:19.
5 See Deuteronomy 15:8.

is really yours, you own it and you occupy the whole thing. And for Jesus to have ownership of our lives, he has to have *all* of our lives. The whole house is his. The old is out and going out. The new is in and coming in. We are made holy to be wholly his.

When we have a right relationship with God, he immediately transforms who we are and whose we are. We are new creations in Christ, and we belong to him. When we live in the right posture of the *yes* position, he continually changes what we do because our lives are open to Jesus taking full ownership of us. He will do his work in every area of our lives. Nothing will be left out because there is no place in our lives he doesn't care about. He wants to have his stamp everywhere, in every room of his house.

After Paul's prayer for the Thessalonians, he offered them encouragement in the promises of God. He said, "The one who calls you is faithful, and he will do it" (1 Thessalonians 5:24). God never stops calling us. For those who are far from him, God is calling them to repent and receive the salvation of Jesus (the oil). For Christians, God is calling them more and more into the *yes* position, removing the old stuff of sin and replacing it with the new stuff of God's holiness. Because God is faithful, we can count on him to come through. Remember, producing holiness in our lives is God's work. We have a role to play, but it's always by his grace.

Where has the *yes* position produced fruit in your life?

_____
_____
_____

In order for Jesus to take full ownership of your life, what elements of your old life still remain that he will need to remove?

_____
_____
_____

In order for Jesus to take full ownership of your life, what new things does he want to move in and set up in you?

_____
_____
_____

What I'm hearing God say to me

Study Day 5

Think of your life as your dream house. Each room matters. Each room is a segment of your personality, your character, your passions, and your desires.

Let's look at the front door. Is it locked or unlocked? God won't force his way in. He must be invited in by faith. That is true when we initially receive salvation in Jesus, but it's also true every day of our lives. To be sanctified or holy is also by grace and through faith. So, are you open to God's work in your life? Are you in the position of inviting him in?

Now move to the kitchen. Everyone is hungry for something. Whatever we hunger after most, we will seek to be the source of our ultimate satisfaction. Throughout history, people have tried everything—power, pleasure, money, fame, etc. None of these things will satisfy. Only when God and the things of God are our ultimate treasure will we be satisfied.[1] That is why it is critical for us to feed off who Jesus is and who we are in him. That is the purpose for regularly nourishing ourselves by God's Word, worship, prayer, sharing in community, service to others, etc. It is through these practices that we are made into *perfect receptors and distributors of the love and glory of God*. So, what are you doing to nourish your soul?

The living room is often the heart of the house. It's where we spend most of our waking time. It's where we are with people the most. Because of that, we definitely want it to be a place of peace. When we are in right relationship with Jesus, we live in the knowledge that "since we have been justified through faith, we have peace with God through our Lord Jesus Christ" (Romans 5:1). That is a precious gift. Peace is not something we are trying to attain; it's something we already have from God by grace. We are wholly his. We don't obey to earn his favor. No, we know we are loved and accepted by God already. We obey, then, as an act of love and thanks to him. So, how does your life reflect the peace you have with God? How does it look more and more like Jesus?

The other room that gets a lot of attention is the bedroom. We make many potentially life-altering decisions involving sex and relationships. We make choices about what we will look at, where we will allow our minds to dwell, and how we will see other people. Added to that, depending on whether we are single or married, we make decisions about appropriate boundaries with others and how relationships should work as a Christian. This includes whether we should even have a relationship with another person at all. When we are wholly his, the Spirit frees us from the cloud of lust and impurity. We are able to see our spouse in the right light and other people as sisters or brothers. So, are your relationships growing in purity?

---
1 See Matthew 13:44.

Now to the study. Our minds control so much of who we are. What we think about right now will very often determine our actions in the future. This is true whether we are thinking about good things or bad things. When Jesus takes full ownership of our lives, he changes our minds. Knowing this, Paul urged, "Do not conform to the pattern of this world, but be transformed by the renewing of your mind" (Romans 12:2). With a new mind, we will begin seeing the world as Jesus does. When we are wholly his, he changes what we think about and how we think about it. So, what does your mind dwell on?

The bathroom is the place we go to get clean. Since we live in a dirty and evil world, it doesn't take much to become tainted by it. When Isaiah realized the depth of his sin in relationship to the holiness of God, he said, "Woe to me...I am ruined! For I am a man of unclean lips, and I live among a people of unclean lips, and my eyes have seen the King, the Lord Almighty" (Isaiah 6:5). What Isaiah knew, and we easily miss, is that he was directly guilty because of his own unclean lips, but he was also indirectly guilty because of his relationship to the unclean lips of the people around him. We are always responsible for our own sin; however, we are also somehow affected because we live in a culture propped up by systemic sin that is all around us. That is why it is so important for us to get clean. In fact, sometimes being wholly his means that the Holy Spirit needs to do some deep cleaning in our lives through ongoing confession and repentance as we are further made aware of places in our lives that do not yet conform to the image of Christ. So, what spiritual deep cleaning needs to be done in your life?

When we know a guest is coming over, and we don't have time to clean the house as we should, where do we put everything? In the closet. The closet is the convenient place to hide the stuff we don't want others to see. It allows us to present the image that everything is nice and tidy, when it's really anything but. Image management is a big temptation for everyone, including Christians. We claim to believe that Jesus knows all of our sin and willingly went to the cross for us still.[2] We claim to live by grace. We even say we desire accountability and transparency before God and with our fellow Christians. Yet sadly, our lives show the opposite. Like Adam and Eve, we hide from God, and we also hide from one another. But when we are wholly his, we are humbled to the core by the depth of our sin while simultaneously finding perfect security in who we are in Jesus, in the reality of his love and acceptance. Because of this, we don't have to hide or pretend anymore, and all the masks of hypocrisy can come off. So, is there something you are hiding that you need to bring into the light?

Finally, we need to move to the garage. Most of our garages have lots of items in them that we have held on to for one reason or another. We saved them at one time, certain that we would need them someday, but we have never used them.

---

2 See Romans 5:8.

Sometimes we can't even remember why we held on to them. We would be better off just throwing most of those things away. Likewise, many of us carry around loads of guilt and shame. We hang on to old memories and old grudges. We beat ourselves up with them, and we use them to beat others up, too. Hanging on to all this stuff often causes bitterness and makes moving forward in Christ impossible.[3] When we are wholly his, he gives us the grace to put aside the things in our past that keep us trapped in the present. So, do you have old stuff stored up that you need to throw away in order to be free?

Pastor Tim Keller argued, "Christians are people who let the reality of Jesus change everything about who they are, how they see, and how they live."[4] Being in right relationship with Jesus and standing with right posture in the *yes* position is how that reality is experienced. We are wholly his, and that is the only way Jesus can take full ownership of our lives. It's the only way he can move into every area of our lives to purify us from sin and set us apart for his service.

To remain steady in the *yes* position, we will always need what John Wesley called the "means of grace." These are "outward signs, words, or actions, ordained of God, and appointed for this end—to be the ordinary channels whereby he might convey to men, preventing, justifying, or sanctifying grace."[5] These practices include "works of piety": regular times of prayer, study of the Scriptures, worship (for Wesley, it also included regular Communion), fasting, and the regular love, accountability, and support of others in the Christian community. They also include regular expressions of individual and corporate obedience to Jesus through what Wesley called "works of mercy." In Wesley's day, these involved doing good; visiting the sick and prisoners; feeding and clothing people; earning, saving, and giving all one could; and opposing slavery.[6] In our day, it may mean directing attention to immigrants in our country, AIDS orphans in Africa, single parents in the inner city, or young people who need to be mentored so they can be successful in reading and math. The possibilities are endless (see Week 7) but, as always, the details of the practices are not as important as the heart motivation behind them. That is why the *yes* position requires engaging in regular practices, deep fellowship, and a life lived out with God's people, our cheerleaders in the fight for holiness.

As we touched on earlier, the world provides no cheerleaders for this kind of life. In fact, the world will be rooting against us. It will be urging us to say *no* to God and the things of God every step of the way. But God is still calling. The Holy Spirit is still working. Every Christian throughout history who has said *yes* is our inspiration and

---

[3] See Hebrews 12:14–15.
[4] Timothy Keller, *The Reason for God* (New York: Riverhead Books, 2008), 241.
[5] John Wesley, "John Wesley's Sermon 'The Means of Grace': A Brief Summary," accessed March 6, 2025, https://kevinmwatson.com/2020/08/04/john-wesleys-sermon-the-means-of-grace-a-brief-summary/#:~:text=Means%20of%20grace%20%E2%80%93%20outward%20signs,and%20receiving%20the%20Lord's%20Supper.
[6] The United Methodist Church, "Means of Grace: Offering mercy, receiving grace," from ResourceUMC, accessed March 6, 2023, https://www.resourceumc.org/en/content/means-of-grace-offering-mercy-receiving-grace.

example. And scores of Christians who are saying *yes* today are our partners along the journey. We are all in this together, as the words of Hebrews 12:1–2 remind us:

> Therefore, since we are surrounded by such a great cloud of witnesses, let us throw off everything that hinders and the sin that so easily entangles. And let us run with perseverance the race marked out for us, fixing our eyes on Jesus, the pioneer and perfecter of faith. For the joy set before him he endured the cross, scorning its shame, and sat down at the right hand of the throne of God.

Probably the most obvious area where the *yes* position takes us is through a relationship rehab.

What do the different rooms in your spiritual house look like? Are they open and occupied by Jesus or polluted by stuff from your old life?

_____
_____
_____

How are you making use of the different "means of grace" in your life? How are you making sure to feed yourself spiritually? Where are you serving others? Where are you stepping out in obedience?

_____
_____
_____

If you went deeper into the *yes* position with God, what would be the visible fruit of that in the next month? How about in the next year? How about ten years from now?

_____
_____
_____

What I'm hearing God say to me

WEEK 4
The Beauty of a Relationship Rehab

Study Day 1

It was a small invader that may have looked cute, but destruction followed directly behind it. It turned a once peaceful environment into absolute chaos in an instant. I'm talking about a squirrel. One managed to get into a house on a summer afternoon in Rochester, New York. The family of five freaked out. It was total pandemonium (think about the movie *National Lampoon's Christmas Vacation*).

What do you do when a squirrel gets into your house? In this case, the brave father rose to the occasion and came up with an excellent plan to banish the invader quickly. He got out the pepper spray.

You can imagine what happened next. Squirrels are small, and they move fast. And this man was no sniper. Before long, total bedlam ensued as the squirrel ran here and there and the entire family was affected by the pepper spray in the air. The fire department was called. All five family members had to have their eyes rinsed by emergency officials. It must have been quite a scene.

Here is my favorite part.

When firefighters came, they opened the windows to air out the house. And guess what happened? The squirrel left. I love the deputy chief's words. He said, "I guess he figured his work there was done."[1]

Talk about trying to fix things the wrong way! Not only was the problem not solved, but many others not directly involved were affected, too. That happens all the time when we get relationships wrong. The effects are deep, and they always spread beyond the two people (or groups) in conflict.

The root of the problem is this: We try to do relationships our way, which really reflects the way of the world and not Jesus' way. Too often the holiness of Jesus that is growing in us simply does not play a role in how we handle relationships, especially when conflict arises in them.

Remember our working definition of holiness? *Holiness is the work of God in us whereby Jesus takes full ownership of our lives, purifies us from sin, and sets us apart for his service.* If Jesus has full ownership of our lives, then he has full ownership of our relationships, too. That means our relationships reflect his holiness more and more because they are marked with the love and glory of God.

Here are just a few of the differences between doing relationships our way versus doing them Jesus' way. When there is a conflict or problem,

---

[1] UPI, "Man uses pepper spray to ward off squirrel," accessed November 9, 2018, https://www.upi.com/Man-uses-pepper-spray-to-ward-off-squirrel/47891212437345/.

- ...our way is to shove it under the rug and pretend everything is okay to minimize the pain. Jesus' way is to acknowledge the true hurt and address the issue in a healthy fashion.
- ...our way is to take revenge in order to make someone else hurt the way he or she hurt us. Jesus' way recognizes that the vicious cycle of revenge never ends; it never satisfies, but true forgiveness does.
- ...our way is to hold a grudge and never let go. Jesus' way is to release the offense so that it no longer controls us.
- ...our way pretends to move on in some kind of peaceful co-existence. Jesus' way tells the truth that a cold war isn't real peace, realizing that only through true forgiveness and mutual reconciliation can peace be fully restored.
- ...our way is to maintain the status quo because it's at least what we know and are used to. Jesus' way is to lead us to the greatest degree of reconciliation possible to the glory of God.
- ...our way is limited to what we can see and know and achieve on our own. Jesus' way is infused with supernatural power and is able to do far more than we could ever ask or imagine.

Jesus teaches mercy, grace, forgiveness, and reconciliation. Unfortunately, too often we accept these as ideals that don't really work. Jesus said that his followers will be known by the love they have for one another and for how they resolve conflict when it comes. Sadly, we act as if he is naïve, he really doesn't understand our situation, and his ways don't work in the real world, but ours do. When we look around, everyone seems to be handling relationships their own way, which is the way of the world in which we live and not Jesus' way. That is the only thing about our way that is actually true. And that's the problem.

Has our approach to relationships actually worked for us? Are we healthier, more whole, or at peace as a result? If we are honest, we would have to say *no* by every measurement. That means we need to change. For practical and personal reasons, we need to do something different. More importantly than that, however, for the sake of the holiness of God and our own growth in it, we must make a change.

Evangelist and author Rebecca Manley Pippert argues, "Holiness, from God's perspective, is intimately connected to how we treat people. Holiness is rooted in relationship."[2] One of the most visible places in which we should be able to see the fruit of Jesus' holiness is in our relationships. That includes each one—from our spouses and children, to our parents and siblings, to extended family, to friends of every stripe, to co-workers and neighbors and even total strangers. **The holiness of Jesus creates and re-creates *shalom* in our lives.**

---
[2] Rebecca Manley Pippert, *Out of the Saltshaker and Into the World* (Downers Grove: InterVarsity Press, 1999), 75.

Shalom is an important biblical word, but not one that we see used in normal conversation. From the Hebrew, *shalom*'s basic meaning is peace, but it's so much bigger than that. It is God's gift of peace and wholeness—body, spirit, and soul—with all of creation through life in him. When *shalom* is present, then everything is as God intended it to be.

Jesus was all about *shalom*. He is total truth and justice, but he is the Redeemer, full of grace and mercy, too. That is why Jesus always taught and lived *shalom* and carried it into every relationship he was ever a part of. To put it succinctly, *shalom* is how the holiness of Jesus is expressed relationally.

Unfortunately, *shalom* hasn't been experienced in the lives of most people today, and this is nothing new. For example, take the first family of Israel—the patriarchs Abraham, Isaac, and Jacob.[3] When you look at that family, you see anything but *shalom*.

Great-Grandpa Abraham and Great-Grandma Sarah were promised by God to have a child who would be the beginning of a new nation. However, as the years rolled by, Abraham turned eighty-six and still had no kids. So they decided to take matters into their own hands. Believe it or not, the idea began with Sarah. She urged Abraham to sleep with her servant, Hagar. Hagar was then to have a child that would be adopted and raised by Sarah as her own. (No, I didn't get this plotline from a daytime television talk show. Although this was common in that time and culture, you don't have to stretch your imagination very far to see the relational damage that might be done.)

As you would expect, this ill-conceived plan only half worked. Abraham and Hagar did sleep together, and she did get pregnant and have a son, but that is where things went off the rails. Raising a child in that kind of dysfunction was just as difficult then as it would be today. In this case, things were complicated even more by the fact that Hagar, the child's real mother, was still around. To add insult to injury, the way she conducted herself was a source of embarrassment and humiliation to Sarah. Fourteen years later, when Abraham was a hundred, they did have their own "promised" child. But regrettably, the division between the two women over their sons was too much. Hagar and her son were exiled from the family. That generation fractured apart with no *shalom*.

In the next generation, Grandpa Isaac and Grandma Rebekah had twin sons. From the beginning, there was a sense of rivalry and competition between the two of them. Isaac favored the oldest, Esau. Rebekah favored the youngest, Jacob. Unbelievably, the parents continued to look the other way as the gulf between the two brothers grew wider and wider. In a climactic scene, Rebekah actually encouraged her favorite, Jacob, to deceive Isaac and steal the all-important blessing from Jacob's

---

[3] This story is told at length in Genesis 12—50.

favorite, Esau. By then, the breach was so severe that Esau wanted Jacob dead. Even after some later attempts at reconciliation, the two brothers were unable to live near each other. That generation also fractured apart with no *shalom*.

In the third generation, Father Jacob had two wives who were also sisters. (I promise this isn't a new reality TV series—go look it up.) Again, this was accepted practice in that time and culture, but despite that, you can see quickly why it didn't go well. Jacob clearly favored one over the other. He even favored some children over others, slept with servant girls, and sparked a rivalry between his sons that led to one being sold into slavery. Like the generations that went before, this one also fractured apart with no *shalom*.

Despite all the different ancient cultural customs and practices that are completely foreign to us in our time, it is clear that this family was filled with dysfunction through and through. All the deceit, favoritism, competition, mistrust, and betrayal simply moved from one generation to the next like a virus, infecting the *shalom* God had intended for them. Every generation fractures apart with no *shalom*.

What they needed was a supernatural relationship rehab. Our lives and our families may not be that upside down and inside out, but we need a relationship rehab, too.

"Holiness, from God's perspective, is intimately connected to how we treat people. Holiness is rooted in relationship."[4] Have you ever considered how your pursuit of holiness is linked to the health of your relationships? How might this change your perspective?

_____

_____

_____

What does it look like internally and externally between two people when *shalom* is present in their relationship? How can outsiders see it?

_____

_____

What does it look like internally and externally between two people when *shalom* is absent? How can outsiders see it?

_____

_____

---

[4] Pippert, 75.

What I'm hearing God say to me

Study Day 2

We all instinctively know when something has gone wrong in a relationship, even if we don't know why or how to fix it. I think we also know that the health of our network of relationships says a lot about us. In fact, as Christians, it's a huge metric of our spiritual health and growth in holiness. Packer said, "The way I relate to others is the essence of my holiness in the sight of God, just as it is one index of it in the sight of men and women."[1]

Now, let's be honest with each other before you read another word. There are people in your life who have hurt you. I know there are people in my life who have hurt me, too.

Most of those hurts are small and relatively insignificant, such as when someone was short or curt with you the other day, but you know that person is going through a rough time and it's out of character for him or her. When that happens, it's frustrating, but you can usually let it go pretty easily. Forgiveness is so simple that it almost seems unnecessary, and reconciliation isn't even needed.

Some hurts may not change your life forever, but they are too big to just ignore. These happen when you get into a fight with your spouse and his or her criticism stings, or when your friend is less than honest with you about something, or when that guy on your ministry team fails to keep his commitment to you—again. These hurts go beyond frustration and usually need some intentional and direct action to resolve. Here, forgiveness requires intentionality, and the reconciliation process is purposeful.

Other hurts are huge and life-altering. When they happen, you know that the relationship is never going to be the same and neither will you. These can come in many forms: betrayal, manipulation, abuse, a verbal or physical assault, you name it. Such hurts must be addressed on many levels and almost always with the help and support of others. Forgiveness takes a long time and hard work. In fact, there are many levels to getting to the place of forgiveness here, and reconciliation is a great challenge that requires new boundaries and relational health in the relationship if it has any hope of continuing. Indeed, the toxic nature of the hurt can be so great that sometimes full reconciliation isn't possible or healthy.

Hurts can come from total strangers or from people very close to us. Perhaps we see these people every day. Maybe we will never see them again. Either way, the hurts are real. They are evidence of the lack of *shalom* between us and others, but we know that Jesus, as a reflection of his holiness, is seeking to create or re-create *shalom* for his glory and our healing.

---

1 Packer, 28.

Since we're being honest with each other, let's take it to the next level. There are people in your life whom you have hurt. I know there are people in my life whom I have hurt, as well.

Just as in the case where we have been hurt, words and actions have caused pain—but in this case the words and actions were ours, and they hurt others. Most of these offenses may be small and getting them right may be as easy as a humble "I'm sorry" said to those whom we hurt. Other times, it may require demonstrating our change of heart beyond words through actions that rebuild trust and promote reconciliation. However, in some of the most serious cases, we will need to have the discipline and guidance of others to help us walk the very difficult road of trying to repair the great damage our words and actions have caused. In those instances, it's usually impossible to make full restitution for the wrongs we committed, but seeking forgiveness and doing our part for reconciliation is still required of us.

Make no mistake: Every time we hurt someone with our words or actions, it is sin. It doesn't matter whether it's severe or not, it is still sin against a holy God and against someone he loves. We cannot gloss over that reality, and we don't want to. Instead, we want to grow in the holiness of Jesus. So whenever we are responsible for the breakdown of *shalom* in a relationship, we must walk the road of repentance in order to create or re-create *shalom* for Jesus' glory and the healing of all involved.

Some people have the mistaken idea that conflict will never happen among Christians. Anyone who has been a Christian for at least a week, however, knows that obviously isn't true. We are fallen people. Even though we are growing in Christ and taking on the characteristics of his holiness, there remain elements of our old nature that we continue to wrestle with. That's why Pastor John Ortberg's advice is so good. He says, "The litmus test of spirituality is not the absence of conflict; conflict will not disappear until we die. The litmus test is how we handle it. Conflict is inevitable. Resentment is optional."[2] Our hunger to experience the fullness of *shalom* in every one of our relationships is a critical aspect of growing in the holiness of Jesus. That is why we fight for it.

In Matthew 5:21, Jesus began addressing broken relationships by stating the obvious: "You have heard that it was said to the people long ago, 'You shall not murder, and anyone who murders will be subject to judgment.' " Everyone knew that it was wrong for God's people to murder someone. Taking away someone's life is an offense that cannot be repaired. And when Jesus said "You have heard that it was said," he was making it clear that his followers agree with and live by the Law of God as stated in the Old Testament. In other words, followers of Jesus will always meet the bare minimum that is required of them by God and others, but that's not even close to all they must do.

---

2 John Ortberg, *Everybody's Normal Till You Get to Know Them* (Grand Rapids: Zondervan, 2003), 138.

Jesus went on to say, "But I tell you that anyone who is angry with a brother or sister will be subject to judgment. Again, anyone who says to a brother or sister, 'Raca,' is answerable to the court. And anyone who says, 'You fool!' will be in danger of the fire of hell" (Matthew 5:22). Jesus was going well beyond the obvious, accepted norms. When he said "But I tell you," he radically deepened and broadened the application of his words, removing all limits and loopholes. He also made it clear that his teaching applies to real life, not just to some religious ritual.

Jesus wasn't just trying to lower the capital punishment stats or asking people to be more civilized. He was getting at the poison that created the murderous spirit in the first place. Anger was the first ingredient of the murderous spirit he brought up.

Of course, there are times when anger can be righteous and appropriate, such as when Jesus himself got angry at all the injustice that was going on in the temple.[3] That is not the kind of anger referenced here, though. Jesus was talking about unrighteous and inappropriate anger. That is the kind of anger where you devalue a person with your comments and don't treat her or him as someone created and loved by God. The person is not your sister or brother, but an enemy to be avoided or defeated. That is the kind of anger that produces a murderous spirit.

Adding to anger is diminishing or dismissing someone with the contemptuous term "Raca," or calling that person a "fool." The root Greek word here for fool is *moros*, which is where we get the English word *moron*. Those may just be words, but words have the power to destroy and produce a murderous spirit, too.

Do you remember the old saying, "Sticks and stones may break my bones, but words will never hurt me"? That is a lie straight from hell itself. Bones heal much faster and more easily than do wounded hearts. Think about it. If you have had a broken bone, it probably healed in a few weeks. But you can still remember painful words spoken to you years ago and, in fact, can still feel the pain afresh right now.

Jesus was saying that anger and name-calling strip away a person's identity as God's beloved creation, replacing it with an ugly wound. Being on the receiving end of anger and name-calling changes your identity and demoralizes you. It makes you feel less like God's beloved creation, worthy of his love and acceptance. It also makes you more likely to do the same to others.

Being on the giving end of anger and name-calling also warps you. As the poison of hatred grows, your life is hollowed out more and more. As former senator Alan Simpson said, "Hatred corrodes the container it's carried in."[4] Anger and name-calling are the poison that creates a murderous spirit. Engaging in them makes us subject to God's judgment.

---

3 See Mark 11:12–19.
4 Alan Simpson, comments made in the eulogy for George H. W. Bush at the National Cathedral in Washington, D.C., December 4, 2018.

We know where this anger comes from: the heart. Our heart determines our thoughts, words, and actions. In another place, Jesus said, "Out of the heart come evil thoughts—murder, adultery, sexual immorality, theft, false testimony, slander. These are what defile a person" (Matthew 15:19–20). When your heart is full of a murderous spirit, you want to kill others, and that is why you are defiled. You may target your enemies first and foremost, but there is almost always collateral damage to the innocent along the way. That is why Jesus offers us a way out and a way back to *shalom*, but it begins at the heart level.

Now, at the heart level, Jesus spelled out how to apply this new relational reality for his followers. First he said, "If you are offering your gift at the altar and there remember that your brother or sister has something against you, leave your gift there in front of the altar. First go and be reconciled to them; then come and offer your gift" (Matthew 5:23–24). Jesus' audience was likely a great distance from the temple in Jerusalem, perhaps as far away as Galilee. The temple was where the altar was. Going there on foot was no small thing and would require lots of time and energy. Jesus was telling them that having his *shalom* in relationships was so important that they needed to leave Jerusalem, go back some distance to home first, get things right, and then return to worship. This would take several days and a lot of effort, but it was that significant. Worship that God wants is not good singing and preaching; it is people who live and walk in *shalom* with one another.

Next Jesus said, "Settle matters quickly with your adversary who is taking you to court. Do it while you are still together on the way, or your adversary may hand you over to the judge, and the judge may hand you over to the officer, and you may be thrown into prison. Truly I tell you, you will not get out until you have paid the last penny" (Matthew 5:25–26). We are to "settle matters quickly" or, literally, to "make friends quickly," because relational debts poison relationships and produce a murderous spirit. Unreconciled anger is the inner equivalent to murder because it is impossible to repay. That sin destroys relationships, when what God wants is people who live and walk in *shalom* with one another.

Jesus' standard here is astonishing. If everyone in the worship service at your church took these words to heart next Sunday, how many people would have to leave? If it was a requirement for admission the next week, how many people couldn't come back?

Jesus attacked the murderous spirit at the core of every breakdown of *shalom*. And his answer was clear: Restore *shalom* quickly and completely. Do it with urgency, action, and authenticity. Don't take your time or hope things just get better on their own. Half measures, fake apologies, and cold wars won't work. Only *shalom* represents and honors the holiness of God.

Take an honest inventory of all your relationships, past and present. Where are there still hurts you are experiencing that are still unresolved?

_____
_____
_____

Now change the focus of your relationship inventory. Where are there places that *you* have caused hurt toward someone else that is still unresolved?

_____
_____
_____

If there are any places where *shalom* is not present in your life, what parts of the brokenness are you responsible for?

_____
_____
_____

What I'm hearing God say to me

Study Day 3

In Matthew 18, Jesus laid out the process for Christians to work out their differences with one another when *shalom* is broken. While Jesus' teaching certainly applies to all of our relationships, it must be understood that some elements of his instruction assume that the relational breach is between fellow Christians who live under his Lordship and who are committed to pursuing his holiness. When relationships with non-Christians are broken, we are still obligated to do everything we can to restore them in a spirit of holiness and love. However, we must recognize that the other side does not claim to live by the values of Jesus; therefore, we should not be surprised if they don't hold to that standard.

Matthew 18 begins with a question about who is the greatest in the Kingdom and ends with a story about a servant who lacked mercy. The main thread throughout each section is what relational *shalom* should look like in the kingdom of God and how we should restore it when it is broken in the world in which we live. We should be like children with a humble love for God.[1] We should be sure not to cause people or ourselves to stumble, especially the immature ones in the faith.[2] We should be sure to care about the children who do fall away from the flock.[3] We should address conflict when it arises, especially when one sins against another, in order to not only bring freedom and restoration to the relationship but also to protect the church from the stain of broken *shalom*.[4] And finally, as people who have received grace and mercy from God, we must be gracious and merciful with others in order to restore *shalom*.[5]

The process Jesus laid out for restoring broken *shalom* is clear, but not easy. He included three important levels, each for a very important reason: personal, partners, and public.

With the personal level (which is probably the only level you can practically go to if you are in conflict with someone who is not a Christian), if someone's "sin" causes an issue with you, you must "go and point out their fault, just between the two of you" (Matthew 18:15). You have a conversation for the purpose of "winning back" your brother or sister and restoring *shalom*. That means you don't set out to win a fight or to exact some kind of revenge. Restoring the relationship is the key here. You go alone because you don't want to embarrass or hurt anyone. Finally, you only go to the person you are at odds with because going to others (unless you are going specifically for advice on how to go directly to the person you are at odds with) only

---

[1] See Matthew 18:1–6.
[2] See Matthew 18:7–9.
[3] See Matthew 18:10–14.
[4] See Matthew 18:15–20.
[5] See Matthew 18:21–35.

makes matters worse and the restoration of *shalom* less likely. You want to "win" the person back, after all.

Sadly, the first level doesn't always work, but that is not an excuse to give up. Jesus said that if going to someone personally does not work, we need to go a second time with a partner or two. The purpose here is the same. We want to "gain" or "win back" our brother or sister. So we are not taking people with us to gang up on anyone; we are taking them to help get all the facts straight, maybe to separate distorted perceptions from the truth and bring clarity to the situation. Notice also that you are still not airing this issue in public because you don't want to embarrass or hurt anyone. Your posture is one of love, and you are humble enough that you yourself might also receive correction and guidance from the third parties in the conversation. Then, even in a worst-case scenario, at least the truth of the matter will be established, even if *shalom* is not restored.

Finally, the third level takes on a much more serious or even disciplinary tone. By the time you reach this point, things have no doubt grown very toxic, and the person on the other side of the relational breach has proven to be hardened against your efforts to restore *shalom*. Because of the other person's posture in levels one and two, this situation has now become a problem for the wider church community, making it public. It's a problem because the sin that has broken down your relationship has probably metastasized into sin that affects other relationships, or at least has the potential to do so if left unchecked. That is why the church, which really means the recognized leaders of the church, now must take on the situation to try to restore *shalom*. Their goal is still the same, which is to win the person back. However, they also have the added responsibility to teach the wider church and protect them from harm. That is why, if the person does not listen, there needs to be a formal break in the relationship with him or her. This is done only as an absolute last resort, and even then the goal is for the person who has broken *shalom* to see the error of his or her ways and return.

This entire process is designed to restore *shalom* when it breaks down. The motivation for doing so is to bring glory to Jesus because *shalom* in our relationships reflects his holiness. *Shalom* is rooted deeply in the fact that we are people of grace and mercy toward one another because we have received abundant grace and mercy from God—again and again and again. In God's economy, grace and mercy go in a straight line, from God to us and then from us to others. That is why Jesus anchored all of this teaching on relationships with the Parable of the Unmerciful Servant.

The parable was actually Jesus' way to answer a question he received from one of his disciples, Peter. Peter asked Jesus, "Lord, how many times shall I forgive my brother or sister who sins against me? Up to seven times?" (Matthew 18:21). On the surface, Peter seemed to be asking a pretty reasonable question and offering a pretty generous answer. He proposed to forgive even without any visible signs of repentance, or even remorse, on the other party's part. He did everything reasonable to forgive—and more, by giving seven chances. That went beyond the minimum standard in the Law, which said he was not to harbor hatred or seek revenge.[6] We could probably accept that. But Jesus' response and Jesus' math took it to an entirely new level. He said, "I tell you, not seven times, but seventy-seven times" (Mathew 18:22). Numbers were not the issue. Jesus was saying that true forgiveness never keeps count. We prefer some version of "three strikes and you're out," but Jesus said forgiveness is a matter of the heart that goes beyond calculation.

To bring the point home, Jesus told a story about a servant who owed the king ten thousand bags of gold or "talents" (from the Greek), a talent being a sum of money and not the ability to sing, play an instrument, or stand on your head. This amount was a ridiculously large sum of money. A single talent was worth roughly twenty years of a day laborer's wages, so ten thousand of them would be the equivalent of billions of dollars in our day. The guy didn't have the money, and sending him to prison may have let the king get some revenge, but it wouldn't get the debt paid. This debt could not ever be paid, and everyone listening knew this.

Still, the servant pleaded for more time, as if it would make a difference. This was like asking for debt consolidation, restructuring, or a short grace period when he was, in fact, bankrupt. He deserved life in prison, but what he needed was mercy, and amazingly that is exactly what he got. The king canceled the debt and set him free.

This king was not normal. He paid a great cost to forgive this debt. Granting mercy always costs someone because mercy is not free. What Jesus didn't explicitly state was implicitly very clear. The king in this story represents God, who paid a great cost to grant his servants mercy. Indeed, the gospel is that Jesus paid our debt of sin at the cost of his own life.

This king acted very weird, but this servant acted very normal. When he ran into another fellow servant just after the amazing cancellation of his own debt, you would expect him to be equally merciful. In this case, his fellow servant owed him a hundred silver coins or "denarii" (from the Greek), a denarius being worth about one day of labor. The amount owed would have been perhaps several thousand dollars in our day. Now, while this debt was real and significant, it could actually be repaid—unlike the first debt. All that was needed was patience and time. Amazingly, this fellow servant used the exact same words the first servant had used before the king, but this time they fell on deaf ears. Indeed, they landed on a heart so cold that, unbelievably, this servant who was just granted great mercy actually threw his fellow servant in prison.

---

[6] See Leviticus 19:17–18.

As expected, word of this exchange got out. Other servants saw and heard about what happened, and they reported the news back to the king. That placed the first servant back in the king's debt and, this time, landed him in prison for life. In case Peter or anyone else might miss his point, Jesus concluded with one of the most powerful lines in all the Scriptures regarding relational *shalom*. He said, "This is how my heavenly Father will treat each of you unless you forgive your brother or sister from your heart" (Matthew 18:35).

Do you appreciate the power of that line? In his holiness, God values *shalom* so much that he said if we refuse to extend mercy to others, he will withhold his mercy from us. A God who forgives us expects and demands that we forgive one another. That should give us all pause and force us to examine the mercy level in our hearts.

God calls us to act in mercy to restore *shalom* for many reasons. First and foremost, we act for Christ's sake, out of love for him and regard for his holiness. We also act for the church's sake, in order to protect the image and integrity of the gospel message. We act for relationship's sake, because we value and love people, including those we have lost *shalom* with. And finally, we act for our own sake because our own well-being and peace are tied to restoring *shalom*.

No matter which side of the relational equation you are on, there is a cost involved in granting forgiveness and restoring *shalom*. If we need to grant forgiveness, we have been offended, and the temptation is to get even somehow or at least to hold a grudge; however, we must pay the cost of surrendering our right to revenge. If we need to receive forgiveness, we have committed some offense, and the temptation is to hold on to our pride and refuse to admit we are wrong; however, we must pay the cost of humbling ourselves and asking for mercy. Only then will God begin to do the supernatural work that restores *shalom* to our relationships.

What is the difference between going to someone in order to win an argument and going to that person with the goal of "gaining" or "winning" your brother or sister back?

_____

_____

Reflecting on your spiritual inventory from Day 2, what is the best way to approach that person who has sinned against you? If it has gone beyond level 1, whom do you need to help you?

_____

_____

How do you need to guard your heart so it doesn't develop the same hardness as that of the servant who refused to forgive his fellow servant?

What I'm hearing God say to me

Study Day 4

It was New Year's Eve 1982 in Fairfax, Virginia, just outside of Washington, D.C. Susan Herzog was eighteen and driving just a mile from her home when she encountered the car of Kevin Tunell, who was seventeen. Susan had been on the road for only three minutes. Kevin had been partying and was very drunk. He was so drunk that friends urged him not to drive, but he bragged, "Nothing will ever happen to me."[1] When he lost control of his car, he smashed into Susan and killed her instantly. He was not even injured.

Susan's parents obviously wanted justice for their daughter, and there was no question that Kevin was guilty. His blood alcohol level was 0.17, well over the legal limit. There were many witnesses, and he didn't deny being at fault. He pled guilty to involuntary manslaughter and drunk driving. Because he was a juvenile and a first-time offender, he was sentenced to three years of probation and one year of community service speaking to different groups about the evils of drinking and driving.

Although nothing could ever be done to bring Susan back and erase the wound that her absence left, her parents didn't believe that was enough justice. So, they took Kevin to court themselves, suing him for $1.5 million for emotional distress.

Doing that was not surprising. But what happened next was.

Both sides agreed to an unusual settlement that no one saw coming. Kevin "would send a check every week to Susan's parents, Lou and Patty Herzog. The check would be made out to their daughter for $1—just a dollar—and he would send it every Friday for 18 years. Susan, the youngest of three daughters, was 18 when she was killed—on a Friday. In all, he would have to pay out exactly $936."[2] The point was that it was weekly, that it forced him to write her name on the check, and that it would go on for a long time.

This seems like it would have been an easy sentence for Kevin, but it wasn't. The burden of guilt soon proved too much for him to bear, and he began missing payments or sending dollar bills instead of checks. Eventually, in 1990, Susan's parents took him back to court to force him to write the checks. Kevin testified through tears, "You get to a point where you kind of snap—and you say, it hurts too much."[3] He offered the Herzogs two boxes of pre-written checks, dated each week through 2001, a year longer than required.

Kevin's contrition moved the judge, but not Susan's parents. Her father, Lou, said,

---

1 Bill Hewitt and Tom Nugent, "Kevin Tunell Is Paying $1 a Week for a Death He Caused and Finding the Price Unexpectedly High," *People*, April 16, 1990, accessed December 14, 2018, https://people.com/archive/kevin-tunell-is-paying-1-a-week-for-a-death-he-caused-and-finding-the-price-unexpectedly-high-vol-33-no-15/.
2 Ibid.
3 Ibid.

"Susan's death is there every waking moment. But every time we don't get a check, there's only one thing that comes to our mind: He doesn't remember."[4] Clutching a folder full of copies of past checks, her mother, Patricia, said, "What we want is to receive that check every week on time. If he does, he will never hear from us.... He must understand we are going to pursue this until August of the year 2000. We will go back to court every month if we have to."[5] They had already gone four times and spent more than four thousand dollars in pursuit of their one-dollar-a-week settlement of $936.

The judge sentenced Kevin to thirty days in jail for not honoring the settlement. And when he got out, he had to keep writing checks. The Herzogs won that day, but did they get justice? I have often wondered how this story ended. After they got their final payment, did they find peace? Kevin was eventually free from legal jeopardy, but was he free from his guilt and shame? Did he ever find peace himself?

That is really the question, isn't it? Every person who is the victim of an offense wants peace. The victim wants *shalom*. The victim doesn't want to hurt anymore, but will he or she pursue peace in light of Jesus and his holiness, or in some other way? Likewise, when an offender comes to terms with his or her offense, the offender wants peace, too. The offender wants *shalom*. The offender wants to be free from the burden of guilt and shame, but will he or she pursue peace in light of Jesus and his holiness, or in some other way?

Three components are laid out in the Scriptures over and over, showing us the road back to *shalom*. We already alluded to them when we looked at Matthew 5 and 18. These three components are repentance, restitution, and reconciliation. But before we go there, we must consider how to seek and honor the holiness of Jesus and pursue *shalom* with others when those components are not present.

As a pastor, I know of far too many situations where this is the case. I personally know families that are broken by abuse and even murder. It's very unlikely, and in some cases impossible, that the offender will take those steps of repentance, restitution, and reconciliation. I know many other situations where the only way the offender will repent is if a bona fide miracle takes place. Some situations are so toxic that victims have had to break contact with the offender just to protect themselves and those they love from further harm. That doesn't even begin to address the reality that many offenders—even those who claim Christ—refuse to surrender their pride in order to walk the road that leads to *shalom*.

What we are honestly saying is that some relationship breaches will not have a happy ending. Even though God intended it and Jesus died to make it possible,

---

4 Ibid.
5 DeNeen L. Brown, "VA. COUPLE WON'T LET DRIVER FORGET KILLING THEIR DAUGHTER," *Washington Post*, March 30, 1990, accessed December 12, 2018, https://www.washingtonpost.com/archive/politics/1990/03/30/va-couple-wont-let-driver-forget-killing-their-daughter/ce55d54a-da0c-46ac-afa7-3f05bd01486d/?noredirect=on&utm_term=.034789b287b8.

sin will prevent *shalom* from being realized. The Bible itself is filled with many such examples because the Bible is real life and not a Disney movie. So, what are we to do if we are the victim, but the offender never seeks to walk the road that leads to *shalom*?

For us, there is the one-way street of forgiveness.

Paul said, "Get rid of all bitterness, rage and anger, brawling and slander, along with every form of malice. Be kind and compassionate to one another, forgiving each other, just as in Christ God forgave you" (Ephesians 4:31–32). This may be a tall order, especially when we really want to reserve our right to get revenge or at least hold a grudge, but it's very clear what God is calling us to do. We are to walk the road of forgiveness even if it's a one-way street.

Before we go any further, it must be said that forgiveness doesn't happen in our own power. We do not have the power to truly forgive people, especially if the offense against us is a serious one. No one does. The power to forgive comes from Jesus. Spiritual formation director James Bryan Smith says it this way: "The only way we can forgive is by letting God renarrate our lives in the context of the metanarrative of Jesus, who forgave his enemies and even died for them. This will lead to healing—the healing of ourselves—which is necessary if we are going to forgive someone who has hurt us."[6] Once Jesus fully inhabits our lives by the Holy Spirit, we can surrender our will to him and forgive those who hurt us.

At the same time, we must acknowledge that forgiveness sometimes gets abused, twisted, and manipulated for evil purposes. Forgiveness doesn't mean that what happened to me didn't really happen. It doesn't mean that it was simply a misunderstanding. And it certainly doesn't mean that it was okay. No! For forgiveness to be real, we have to be clear that a wrong was committed: I was violated somehow; it was unjust, mean, and evil; it's clear and I know it, even if the offender won't admit it. Forgiveness happens when I clearly acknowledge the wrong, but then I give up my right to hurt that person for hurting me.

And forgiveness isn't a feeling, either. If it were a feeling, we would never forgive. I can't think of a time when I have been really hurt by someone that I ever felt like forgiving him or her, at least at first. Forgiveness is not a feeling; it is first and foremost an act of the will. We are obeying Jesus by granting a pardon to the one who offended us. This person is still guilty of the offense, but we are releasing him or her from the punishing response that person deserves.

It is obvious that forgiveness has benefits to the offender in that he or she receives a pardon from us. However, it benefits us a great degree, too. To refuse to forgive

---

6 James Bryan Smith, *The Good and Beautiful Community* (Downers Grove: InterVarsity Press, 2010), 110.

is to allow all the poison of bitterness, wrath, anger, clamor, slander, and malice that Paul warned against to live in our lives.

Imagine you have an IV strapped to your arm, slowly administering poison. Every moment the IV is in your arm, you are going to get sicker and sicker until you eventually die. Forgiveness is like taking the IV out of your arm. Forgiveness is good for *you*. Perhaps author Lewis Smedes said it best: "To forgive is to set a prisoner free and discover that the prisoner was you."[7]

Paul's words offer more helpful guidance to us beyond taking the steps to forgive. He wrote, "Do not repay anyone evil for evil. Be careful to do what is right in the eyes of everyone. If it is possible, as far as it depends on you, live at peace with everyone" (Romans 12:17–18). There are two clear and simple lines that we cannot cross. First, we are never justified in doing evil to someone else. It's just a non-negotiable thing for us as Christians. Jesus' holiness demands that we cannot embrace words, actions, or even thoughts designed to hurt those who have hurt us.

Second, we are always responsible to control ourselves and do our part for peace. This means that, even though we cannot control others, we can control ourselves. And because we can control ourselves, out of regard for the holiness of Jesus we want to make sure our posture is open for peace whenever that one-way street of forgiveness can turn into a two-way street of repentance, restitution, and reconciliation that leads to *shalom*.

If you have been hurt by someone, what does forgiveness look like? How many payments do you require?

_____
_____
_____

How does forgiveness have to be an act of the will instead of a feeling? How does it have to be supernatural instead of something done in your power?

_____
_____
_____

---

7 Lewis Smedes, "Lewis B. Smedes > Quotes > Quotable Quote," *Goodreads*, accessed December 21, 2018, https://www.goodreads.com/quotes/166122-to-forgive-is-to-set-a-prisoner-free-and-discover.

Is there someone you need to forgive whom you have withheld forgiveness from? What will it take to begin the process of releasing that pain and poison by forgiving?

_____
_____
_____
_____

What I'm hearing God say to me

_____
_____
_____
_____
_____
_____
_____
_____
_____
_____
_____
_____
_____
_____
_____
_____
_____
_____
_____
_____
_____
_____
_____

week 4 day 4

Study Day 5

Now let's look at the two-way street.

First, let's dig into how repentance contributes to the creation or re-creation of *shalom*. In Week 2, we said that repentance is *the Holy Spirit–produced sorrow over sin that leads to confession, contrition, and a direct change in the course of our lives from sin to God*. When it comes to relationships and repairing the brokenness of *shalom*, genuine repentance often has many dimensions. But how do you know if it's real?

I remember counseling a married couple that was in serious trouble. They had been separated for a time, and both spouses were very angry for various reasons. At some point during the separation, the husband had slept with an ex-girlfriend. His wife was understandably devastated and struggled with the pain and deep sense of betrayal that go with adultery. This couple had come to me because the wife wanted to try to save their marriage but, for that to happen, things needed to change and trust needed to be rebuilt. Even though she wasn't using the word, she was asking for repentance from her husband.

The husband's guilt was not in doubt. He acknowledged the fact that he had committed adultery. He even said that he was sorry and wanted to save their marriage. Sadly, though, he didn't want to deal with the consequences of his actions and the ongoing work he was going to have to do to make restitution for his sin and reconcile with his wife. At one point in our session, he blurted out a line that I will never forget: "I said I was sorry. Why don't you just forget about it and let it go?!" He may have had regret over his actions, but he clearly didn't have repentance.

So, how do you know when genuine repentance is present? Pastor Steve Cornell says a person who "is genuinely repentant:

1. Accepts full responsibility for his or her actions….
2. Welcomes accountability from others.
3. Does not continue in the hurtful behavior or anything associated with it.
4. Does not have a defensive attitude about being in the wrong.
5. Does not dismiss or downplay the hurtful behavior.
6. Does not resent doubts about their sincerity or the need to demonstrate sincerity—especially in cases involving repeated offenses.
7. Makes restitution where necessary."[1]

---

[1] Steve Cornell, "How to Move from Forgiveness to Reconciliation," *The Gospel Coalition*, accessed December 14, 2018, https://www.thegospelcoalition.org/article/how-to-move-from-forgiveness-to-reconciliation/.

The differences between someone who takes on these attributes and that adulterous husband in my office are obvious. You can see them plainly because the former's words match a new attitude that is backed up with very different actions over time, with a greater offense often taking a longer time for the new attitude to take root.

If you are the offender, repentance is the first step for you. Don't just feel bad about your sin. Confess it to God and seek his forgiveness. Then, out of your changed heart, confess your sin to the one you offended and seek that person's forgiveness. Finally, no matter how the one you offended responds, turn from your sinful ways to pursue the holiness of Jesus, which includes the next two steps on the road to *shalom*.

If you are the victim, repentance is the first step that your offender must take, but it's not the last. It's important at this point for you to acknowledge your offender's change of heart. Extend grace and mercy to him or her as much as possible and make your forgiveness clear. At the same time, you can point out your ongoing sense of uneasiness about the relationship, if there is any, or even your lack of trust about his or her intentions. It's okay to be honest, but try to be fair, too. You may even do your offender the service of spelling out what else you need to see happen for you to begin rebuilding trust in the relationship, setting real metrics for restitution.

That brings us to the second step on the road to *shalom*, restitution. Restitution means that the offender does whatever is possible to repay the victim for the wrong that has been done. It's about trying to put things back together the way they were before the offense occurred. Perhaps one of the best examples of restitution is found in the Gospel of Luke with the story of Zacchaeus.[2]

Zacchaeus was a tax collector in a time when tax collectors extorted money and property from people. We don't know the full extent of his sin, but it seems that it was big. We also know that, when he met Jesus, he clearly and publicly repented of his sin. Then he began to take the next logical step of restitution. In fact, he went way beyond what was required. He said, "Look, Lord! Here and now I give half of my possessions to the poor, and if I have cheated anybody out of anything, I will pay back four times the amount" (Luke 19:8). I've often wondered what it must have looked like for him to go door to door performing one act of restitution after another. His initial embrace of Jesus probably got him a lot of eye rolls and scoffs, but his restitution must have blown people away. Zacchaeus put his money where his mouth was.

Restitution turns our words of repentance into actions that bring healing to the ones we have hurt. In cases such as that of Zacchaeus, making restitution is pretty cut and dried: What was taken must be returned. However, it is not always that easy. For example, when a reputation has been damaged due to gossip and lies, how can full restitution be made? It's impossible to make sure that everyone will now hear the truth. When someone is betrayed or taken advantage of, what will restitution look

---
2 See Luke 19: 1–10.

like there? Worse yet, how can you make restitution when a life has been taken? Those acts cannot somehow be undone. We could go on listing more examples of how restitution usually isn't a simple measure of spiritual accounting, but Zacchaeus's example still helps us.

You can imagine that Zacchaeus's many sins couldn't just be fixed with the return of ill-gotten money. When he took more than he should have from Fred the farmer, it might have caused Fred to miss out on a needed business opportunity with Sam the shepherd. And that doesn't include Mike the merchant, who didn't have the money to care for his sick child who subsequently died, or Frank the fisherman, who lost his business when he couldn't pay the note on his boat. That is why it is beautiful to consider the lengths to which Zacchaeus was willing to go in his restitution. He was giving back to people four times more than he took! Fred and Sam still missed out on their business deal, Mike's child was still tragically dead, and Frank still lost his boat—those things could not be undone. But what *was* being done by Zacchaeus demonstrated a good-faith effort to do everything in his power to repair the extended damage he had caused. That is often where we see the redemptive power of restitution the most.

In each situation, restitution may look very different. There is no one-size-fits-all approach. Making restitution is about the offender sharing his or her changed heart with the victim in tangible and practical ways. Seeing words of repentance matched up with a new attitude and backed up with actions designed to restore what has been broken will speak volumes. It has the great potential to apply the healing power of God to the brokenness of sin. It also reflects the holiness of Jesus and the *shalom* he wants to restore to our relationships.

We should also distinguish the difference between restitution in the case of private sin and restitution in the case of public sin. When sin is committed against someone privately, such as a harsh criticism, restitution might include a heartfelt apology and a private but meaningful gesture of love that leads to peace. Yet when that same harsh word is given publicly, or when it is spread around through gossip over time, restitution might require a public apology followed by actions done to restore the reputation or image of the victim. Perhaps those gestures of love that lead to peace must go above and beyond for no other reason than to demonstrate the offender's sincerity to the victim and to the others who saw the offense that was committed.

If you are the offender, restitution is critical. Your words of repentance and new attitude are not enough. They must be coupled with actions designed to restore what is broken or lost. Sometimes those actions are obvious, such as returning something that was stolen. Other times, restitution needs to be more creative, especially when the victim is less than open to your acts of repentance. Put simply, you must do whatever is reasonable and within your power to right the wrong you have committed, even if the one you offended refuses to accept it. In that regard, restitution is not only about trying to restore *shalom* but also about glorifying a holy God.

If you are the victim, restitution is the time when you will begin to witness the changed heart of the one who offended you. You should be able to see your offender trying to make things right as best he or she can. Believe it or not, your offender won't always know what to do. While it may be obvious to you, it's just not obvious to him or her. So help your offender in a spirit of gentleness. Tell him or her what restitution should look like to you, but be sure to make it something that is achievable, and don't be afraid to clarify that things will still take time. While restitution can and should begin immediately after repentance, it may take days, weeks, or even years to see its full effects. How your offender begins making restitution and how you receive it will set the tone and the overall course for reconciliation.

Reconciliation is the third step on the road to *shalom*. People often merge forgiveness and reconciliation and assume they are the same thing. They are not. While forgiveness can, and sometimes must be, a one-way street, reconciliation is always a two-way street. It has to be. Reconciliation is the complete restoration of the broken relationship to health and peace. In other words, *shalom* is restored. However, reconciliation is completely contingent on the attitude and actions of both parties.

Make no mistake, reconciliation is difficult. It takes a lot of humility and commitment to the other person. It also takes a lot of time. And truth be told, we usually don't want to make the investment. Pastor Philip Nation explains, "When things get hard, it is the natural inclination to just wash our hands of others. Those with power and prestige say it is not just acceptable but expected to wash your hands of difficult situations. People are messy. In fact, they often drag me into their own mess."[3] Here, more than at any other time on the road to *shalom*, we have to make sure, again and again, that we are committed to the way of Jesus.

Jesus' holiness demands that we pursue reconciliation to the greatest degree possible, for his glory first and also for our healing. As the writer of Hebrews admonished, "Make every effort to live in peace with everyone and to be holy; without holiness no one will see the Lord. See to it that no one falls short of the grace of God and that no bitter root grows up to cause trouble and defile many" (Hebrews 12:14–15). Reconciliation always honors God. It always reflects his holiness.

There are many examples of reconciliation in the Bible, including accounts of times when it did not occur and the damage that resulted. One of the most interesting comes at the tail end of the Book of Philippians. As Paul was closing out his letter to the church in Philippi, he made a personal appeal to two women. Here is what he said: "I plead with Euodia and I plead with Syntyche to be of the same mind in the Lord. Yes, and I ask you, my true companion, help these women since they have

---
[3] Philip Nation, *Habits for Our Holiness* (Chicago: Moody Publishers, 2016),155.

contended at my side in the cause of the gospel, along with Clement and the rest of my co-workers, whose names are in the book of life" (Philippians 4:2–3). Something had gone wrong between these two women. It wasn't rooted in some overt sin or bad doctrine, or Paul would have corrected them. It was some kind of relational issue.

Maybe it was something such as Euodia having a party and inviting other women but not inviting Syntyche, who assumed a slight and was now giving Euodia the cold shoulder. Or perhaps Euodia didn't get asked to sing on the worship team and Syntyche did, and now Euodia was jealous. Maybe Euodia had a sharp tone with Syntyche, which made her so mad that she was telling everyone about it and even hinting about it on Facebook. Perhaps Syntyche asked for help with a problem and felt that Euodia didn't jump fast enough or go far enough. The possibilities are endless, but it must have looked like some first-century version of that.

So, how would it get fixed? How could the women reconcile? Earlier in his letter, Paul appealed to the whole church to have the "same mind" in the way they related to one another. He wrote, "If you have any encouragement from being united with Christ, if any comfort from his love, if any common sharing in the Spirit, if any tenderness and compassion, then make my joy complete by being like-minded, having the same love, being one in spirit and of one mind" (Philippians 2:1–2). The basis for that "same mindedness" was, of course, the humility exemplified in a holy Jesus.[4] He was their ultimate example.

In what way were these women to have the "same mind"? They needed to remember that they both belonged to Jesus. They were spiritual sisters. That connection was the bridge to reconciliation and love. Jesus was and had to be the source for the return of *shalom* to their relationship; they must submit their hearts to him. Again, Philip Nation explains, "Submission is not about being subhuman or loathing ourselves. It is finding our true worth in the relationship forged by the cross and empty tomb. In your daily discipline of relinquishing power to Jesus and living with the accountability of friends in the faith, you will find love. It is the love that dies for you and gives all for your holiness."[5] Their hearts would be softened as they submitted to Jesus and remembered who they were in him.

Paul also said that these women needed the help of a "true companion." A true companion is a third party who has credibility with both sides. This third party can see things that one side or the other cannot see. As a result, a "true companion" can identify places where the old relationship was unhealthy, even toxic, and point out what a new relationship with Jesus' *shalom* might look like.

The third party can also say things that need to be said even when one side (or both) doesn't want to hear them. Because of that person's authority and perspective,

---

4 See Philippians 2:5.
5 Nation, 180.

he or she can be Jesus' agent in the relationship to broker peace in whatever form is best for the future. This "true companion" influence is huge because, if the conflict is serious, it's almost always necessary to have outside help if reconciliation is ever going to happen.

If you are the offender, reconciliation should be your deep desire. You have already uttered words of repentance, displayed a new attitude, and begun backing all that up with actions or restitution. Now you must keep that going by seeking the greatest level of peace possible. A "true companion" can help you. Resist the temptation to go it alone, and instead do the hard work of submitting to that person as he or she points you to Christ. Do it even when it's hard—because it will be hard. Even in the best of situations, the new relationship will probably not look like the old one. It shouldn't, anyway. You need to maintain an open and soft posture that is willing to take the next step as soon as the victim is. The victim is often the one who needs to determine the pace of reconciliation. What that person needs to see from you, more than anything else, is consistency and humility in line with your previous words and actions.

If you are the victim, reconciliation should be your deep desire, too. Obviously, it is the responsibility of the offender to do much of the heavy lifting, but you must continue to be merciful and gracious if your offender is ever going to have a chance.

You may be nervous and afraid to invite new and further pain into your life. You may think that any new relationship with the offender is destined to look just like the old one did. That's possible, but it doesn't have to be that way. In fact, if you bring a "true companion" into this process, that person can help you see places where you need to own your part in the problems of the past. A true companion can also protect you by helping you to build good relational boundaries for the future.

Of course you, too, must be open and softhearted for the process to move forward, but know that you are setting the pace for how this works. Know also that every action designed to bring peace always brings glory to God.

Have you ever suffered from chronic headaches? Li Fuyan did for more than four years. He tried every treatment imaginable. Nothing helped. Then an X-ray finally revealed why. He had a rusty, four-inch knife blade lodged in his skull. It had been there ever since he was attacked by a robber. He knew that he had suffered lacerations on the right side of his jaw, but he didn't know the blade had broken off inside his head. Amazingly, he suffered unnecessarily for four years because of it.[6]

Just as you can't live with a foreign object buried in your body, you can't live with relational brokenness in your soul. It must be removed. But none of this is possible without the supernatural power of the Holy Spirit. We can't do this on our own.

---

[6] "Chinese doctors remove rusty blade stuck in man's skull for four years," The Guardian, accessed December 21, 2018, https://www.theguardian.com/world/2011/feb/18/china-knife-blade-skull-surgery.

Saint Ignatius of Loyola once prayed, "Lord, I freely yield to You all my liberty, Take my memory, my intellect, and my entire will. You have given me everything I am or have; I give it all back to You to stand under Your will alone. Your love and Your grace are enough for me, I ask for nothing more."[7] This is a picture of surrender to God and of the laying down of our rights and privileges for his glory. *Shalom* requires just that. That is why we forgive when we are offended. That is why we seek forgiveness when we offend others. And it's why we walk the important road of *shalom*, paved with repentance, restitution, and reconciliation.

What is the difference between forgiveness and reconciliation? How can you make sure not to conflate or confuse them?

_____
_____
_____

Is there a place where you have offended someone and you know you need to repent? What is the best way to repent clearly and directly to that person?

_____
_____
_____

Is there some restitution you need to make for a past wrong? What is the most redemptive way to take those steps?

_____
_____
_____

Is there a relationship you need to reconcile? What is the most healthy way to do that, and what is the greatest level of reconciliation you are responsible for on your end?

_____
_____
_____

---

7 Peter Kreeft, *Prayer: The Great Conversation* (San Francisco: Ignatius Press, 1991), 172.

What I'm hearing God say to me

WEEK 5
Overcoming in the Hard Times

Study Day 1

We all have those seasons of life that we will never forget.

October 2018 was one of those times for me.

My mom had been struggling with some health issues off and on since the summer. On the last day of September—a Sunday—she went back into the hospital to try to get a handle on an infection that was causing all kinds of other complications in her body.

We talked on the phone that day. She felt very discouraged and sick. The hospital was the last place she wanted to be, but it was where she needed to be. On Tuesday, they decided to transfer her to a larger hospital about an hour away from home. She hated that idea even more, but she went along because there were no other options. I talked to her that day, too. She asked that I pray for God to heal her so she wouldn't have to go. I did, but I also prayed that the doctors would find the answers she needed. Little did I know that would be the last time I spoke to my mom.

On Wednesday and Thursday, I talked to my dad, but my mom just didn't feel up to talking. On Thursday afternoon, her nurse explained the course of treatment they were going to do. She sounded confident, and it seemed straightforward to me. They even sent my dad home for the night. Four hours later, my mom was dead.

I was in a church meeting in Texas, nearly one thousand miles away from their home in Illinois. There was nothing I could do, and the shock was overwhelming. I was the first one to hear the official news from the doctors that she had crashed and they couldn't bring her back. I was the one who had to call my dad and tell him the news as he was rushing back to the hospital. I had to call my brother at work, who was just as shocked as I was. Then I had to drive home and tell my wife and kids. It was the first close family death my children had ever experienced.

As a pastor, I have been with families around death and funerals more times than I can remember, but this was the first time in my adult life that I was part of the grieving family. I never expected my mom to die so quickly. My stomach was upset. I couldn't think clearly. I didn't sleep well at all that night. My mind was racing, but not in any particular direction.

The next morning, I found myself on a plane to go be with my dad and began making all the arrangements for funerals and futures following an unexpected death. For many days, we worked through financial papers and legal documents to help my dad move forward. We worked to clean up and clean out the house so he could live there more comfortably by himself. To add to the chaos, because of a series of unfortunate circumstances, I found myself in the position of having to plan and lead my own mother's funeral because her pastor was unavailable. To say that the week was stressful is an understatement.

That wasn't the only grief I had to walk through, though. The day I flew home to Houston, about four hours after my plane landed, I was called to the hospital because one of my good friends had surprisingly coded when he went to the ER with back pain. I rushed to his side to be with his wife and family as he passed away. A second funeral now lay before me and another surprising loss of someone I loved.

Of course, that wasn't everything. There was an interview weekend scheduled for an open staff position at the church I pastored the day after my mom passed. Even though I wasn't present, there were things I had to do to hand off those responsibilities and work I had to do to process what went on while I was away.

Then there was a trip to Portland for a meeting I had to attend.

A weekend of interviews for a second pastoral candidate.

A previously scheduled surgery.

Our church hosted our state assembly meeting.

And still tucked into all of that were all the normal responsibilities of life.

That was October 2018.

Suffering comes in all shapes, sizes, and durations. I know that what I experienced was nothing compared to what others have endured or are enduring. But one thing is for sure when it comes to suffering: it is not a contest. Just because one person's suffering is greater or lasts longer doesn't invalidate or minimize the suffering of someone else.

Suffering is real. Suffering is unfair. Suffering is common. Suffering is unavoidable. Suffering can even be overwhelming. But suffering can be used by God to conform us more to the image of Jesus and increase the measure of his holiness in us.

Suffering takes on many shapes and sizes, and it happens for many reasons. It can come as a result of our own personal bad choices. In other words, our sin or lack of wisdom brings on pain. Suffering can come because of the evil and destructive actions of others. We may not like to admit it, but we are often victims of what other people do to us. People suffer because they experience a great loss. Whether it is the loss of a loved one or of something very special to us, going through loss can be very difficult. Maybe most distressing of all, however, suffering happens to us because of forces outside of our control or beyond our understanding. In other words, we can go through suffering with no clear answer as to why.

Tim Keller reflected on suffering this way:

> No matter what precautions we take, no matter how well we have put together a good life, no matter how hard we have worked to be healthy, wealthy, comfortable with friends and family, and successful with our career—something will inevitably ruin it. No amount of money, power, and planning can prevent bereavement, dire illness, relationship betrayal, financial disaster, or a host of other troubles from entering your life. Human life is fatally fragile and subject to forces beyond our power to manage. Life is tragic.[1]

The Bible does not hide from the problem of suffering. In fact, we see the reality of suffering and the assurance of God's presence and help in the midst of suffering from cover to cover. Think of Jonah or David, who suffered because of their bad choices. Think of Jeremiah or Paul, who suffered because of the evil done to them by others. Think of Mary and Martha, who walked through grief and loss. And, of course, think of Job, who went through a season of terrible suffering that was outside of his control or understanding. Those are just some examples.

God's Word provides a message of hope to God's people who endure suffering—not so they will avoid or even minimize it, but so they "do not grieve like the rest of mankind, who have no hope" (1 Thessalonians 4:13). Keller stated, "While other worldviews lead us to sit in the midst of life's joys, foreseeing coming sorrows, Christianity empowers people to sit in the midst of the world's sorrows, tasting the coming joy."[2]

Because of Jesus' victory over sin and death, no suffering we experience, no matter what the origin or severity, can ever have the last word. Because of the power of the Holy Spirit that now inhabits our lives through Christ, even our suffering can have meaning and purpose and be useful in making us holy by conforming us to the image of Christ. It's not that suffering leads to holiness or that we can't lead a holy life apart from suffering, but that even suffering can have value as we pursue a holy life. That is our hope as Christians.

As we have said over and over now: *Holiness is the work of God in us whereby Jesus takes full ownership of our lives, purifies us from sin, and sets us apart for his service.* This means that there is spiritual work to be done in our lives even when we suffer. In fact, it further reiterates the truth that God cares more about our holiness than he does our happiness. That is his ultimate purpose for us. **When we fight for the holiness of Jesus in our lives, even when we suffer, we come to live by the hope that Jesus overcame so that we can overcome.**

---

1 Timothy Keller, *Walking with God Through Pain and Suffering* (New York: Penguin Group, 2013), 3.
2 Ibid., 31.

To what degree do you think most people accept that suffering is inevitable for all of us? Why?

_____
_____
_____

Why are we so surprised when suffering actually comes our way? What does this say about how much we really pay attention to what the Bible says about suffering?

_____
_____
_____

How can God use our pain to help us grow spiritually?

_____
_____
_____

What I'm hearing God say to me

Study Day 2

Christians who fight for holiness in the midst of suffering are overcomers. The word *overcome* (also translated as "conquer," "victorious," or "triumph") is a powerful term in the New Testament, especially as used by John. In his first Epistle, John wrote, "Everyone born of God overcomes the world. This is the victory that has overcome the world, even our faith. Who is it that overcomes the world? Only the one who believes that Jesus is the Son of God" (1 John 5:4–5). We can overcome everything in the world, its evil and sin as well as its suffering and pain, because of Jesus. Jesus overcame so that we can overcome.

In the Book of Revelation, being an overcomer becomes much more visible. In every one of the promises Jesus made to the seven churches of Revelation 2 and 3, there is a reward for those who are victorious or overcome. Let me list them briefly:

- "To the one who is victorious, I will give the right to eat from the tree of life, which is in the paradise of God" (Revelation 2:7).
- "The one who is victorious will not be hurt at all by the second death" (Revelation 2:11).
- "To the one who is victorious, I will give some of the hidden manna. I will also give that person a white stone with a new name written on it, known only to the one who receives it" (Revelation 2:17).
- "To the one who is victorious and does my will to the end, I will give authority over the nations—that one 'will rule them with an iron scepter and will dash them to pieces like pottery'—just as I have received authority from my Father. I will also give that one the morning star" (Revelation 2:26–28).
- "The one who is victorious will…be dressed in white. I will never blot out the name of that person from the book of life, but will acknowledge that name before my Father and his angels" (Revelation 3:5).
- "The one who is victorious I will make a pillar in the temple of my God. Never again will they leave it. I will write on them the name of my God and the name of the city of my God, the new Jerusalem, which is coming down out of heaven from my God; and I will also write on them my new name" (Revelation 3:12).
- "To the one who is victorious, I will give the right to sit with me on my throne, just as I was victorious and sat down with my Father on his throne" (Revelation 3:21).

These are wonderful promises from God. They are greater than we can even imagine from the limits of our human senses and perspective. They are not limited by time and space. They are not bound by any power of any kind on this earth.

These promises take on even more depth and meaning when we realize the context of the Book of Revelation. God's people were suffering greatly, either being persecuted for their faith or living under imminent threat of it. In the wider Roman culture, they were asked to declare Caesar as Lord and renounce Jesus as Lord while constantly being tempted to be like the rest of the world around them sexually, socially, economically, and religiously. To not conform to the pressures of the world around them brought them great suffering. Beyond that, they still suffered from everything common to humans: sickness, death, being victim to natural disasters, etc.[1]

The only way they were going to endure under all this pressure was to look to Jesus, who overcame so they could overcome. But what would that mean? How would they overcome? Later in the book, John described the believers' struggle with the devil, saying, "They triumphed over him by the blood of the Lamb and by the word of their testimony; they did not love their lives so much as to shrink from death" (Revelation 12:11). That is the means by which we overcome.

Overcoming by the blood of the Lamb means overcoming by our faith in Jesus. It is about what Jesus has done, not what we do. In that way, we don't win victory but claim it by faith in Christ.

Jerry Bridges, who was a Christian author, speaker, and staff member at the Navigators, explained, "Faith is not only necessary to salvation, it is also necessary to live a life pleasing to God. Faith enables us to claim the promises of God—but it also enables us to obey the commands of God. Faith enables us to obey when obedience is costly or seems unreasonable to the natural mind."[2] Overcomers trust in the blood of the Lamb and not in their own goodness. Because of that trust, they obey Jesus even when it's hard. Jesus overcame so they can overcome.

Overcoming by the word of our testimony means overcoming by our faithfulness to Jesus. In the first-century Roman world, that meant publicly claiming Jesus was Lord instead of Caesar, and worshiping him no matter what. That would cost them their jobs, their property, their relationships, and maybe even their lives. Can you see the weight of suffering they were taking on?

Overcoming by the word of their testimony also meant they would model a life under the Lordship of Jesus, which would look very different from the lives of those who were not his. As they loved and served others in Jesus' name, people would see their life under Christ. As they suffered for Christ without evil or reproach, people would see their ultimate allegiance to Jesus.

---

1 For further background on the historical context of Revelation 2 and 3, see T. Scott Daniels, *Seven Deadly Spirits: The Message of Revelation's Letters for Today's Church* (Grand Rapids: Baker Academic, 2009) or N. T. Wright, *Revelation for Everyone* (Louisville: Westminster John Knox Press, 2011).
2 Jerry Bridges, *The Pursuit of Holiness* (Colorado Springs: NavPress, 2006), 110.

To be an overcomer by the blood of the Lamb and the word of our testimony, we have to prepare our minds for the reality and inevitability of suffering. Perhaps one of the biggest roadblocks to being an overcomer is the sheer shock and surprise that suffering even comes upon us in the first place. Peter wrote, "Dear friends, do not be surprised at the fiery ordeal that has come on you to test you, as though something strange were happening to you. But rejoice inasmuch as you participate in the sufferings of Christ, so that you may be overjoyed when his glory is revealed" (1 Peter 4:12–13).

Paul was also blunt, stating, "Everyone who wants to live a godly life in Christ Jesus will be persecuted" (2 Timothy 3:12). Because of this reality, we need to prepare our minds before the suffering comes. We must ground ourselves in the truth of the Scriptures and the eternal promises of God (such as those we saw in Revelation 2 and 3). If we don't know them and don't stay rooted in them, it will be easy to be washed away when the tidal wave of suffering hits.

Overcoming by the blood of the Lamb and the word of our testimony concerns more than knowledge. It is also a matter of the heart. Our hearts must be rooted and grounded in the love of Christ. We must be actively dependent upon him in prayer. David said, "You, LORD, are a shield around me, my glory, the One who lifts my head high" (Psalm 3:3). God must be so real to us, so close, so personal that he can indeed be our shield. Pleasing him must be the focal point of our lives because he is our glory. And he must be the one who lifts our head out of despair.

When you know God in that way, you can look up to him with the right eyes. As the psalmist said, "I lift up my eyes to the mountains—where does my help come from? My help comes from the LORD, the Maker of heaven and earth" (Psalm 121:1–2). God is good, and he is the only one who can really care for us, especially when we are suffering. As we pray, we can look up to a God whom we know is looking out for us.

We prepare our minds and hearts now because we know that suffering could arrive in the next five minutes or five years. In any event, we need to be ready. Being ready means being more and more conformed to Jesus. We know that God has made us his in Christ, by grace and through our faith. We also know that because we are now his, it is God's will that we would be made holy like Jesus.

Paul wrote, "And we know that in all things God works for the good of those who love him, who have been called according to his purpose. For those God foreknew he also predestined to be conformed to the image of his Son, that he might be the firstborn among many brothers and sisters" (Romans 8:28–29). Being "conformed" to Jesus is God's ultimate purpose for us. That is the good. That is what we are called to. It is why Jesus pursued us even when he foreknew all of our sin. It is what we are predestined for. It is what the Holy Spirit is leading us to, being conformed to Jesus.

Being conformed to Jesus means we are going to be shaped by his character in all things. It means being shaped by Jesus' words and actions that are becoming more and more visible in our lives. It also means being shaped by Jesus' suffering and death. In Christ, the bad things will work out for good, the truly good things cannot be taken away, and the best things are yet to come.[3] Because Jesus overcame, we can overcome.

Given all the suffering and trials that the original audience of Revelation were enduring or might have come to them, why was it so important to hammer home the need for them to be overcomers?

_____
_____
_____

What specific challenges are you currently facing that require an overcoming faith?

_____
_____
_____

How does the promise of a reward from Jesus encourage you to persevere in the trials you are facing now or might face some day?

_____
_____
_____

---

[3] Adapted from Jonathan Edwards, "Christian Happiness," in *The Works of Jonathan Edwards: Sermons and Discourses 1720–1723*, vol. 10, ed. Wilson H. Kimnach (New Haven, CT: Yale University Press, 1992), 297.

What I'm hearing God say to me

Study Day 3

As overcomers in Jesus, we increasingly become victors over the monsters in and around us. These monsters can be the reason we suffer, the outgrowth of our suffering, or just a byproduct of our suffering. There are many different types of monsters, but some examples include guilt, shame, hurt, disappointment, loneliness, sickness, and anger. One thing they all have in common is pain.

Pain and suffering are often one and the same. We are pained because of the guilt of our actions. The dark label of shame on us is a constant source of pain. Our hurts and disappointments cause pain. Experiencing deep loneliness is painful. When we are sick, especially with chronic or terminal illness, the pain can go beyond the physical to encompass many different dimensions. Even anger is often a result of a reaction or overreaction to pain.

So, how can we overcome these monsters? By knowing, in our heads and in our hearts, that Jesus did not abandon us in all of his pain and, therefore, he won't abandon us in the midst of ours.

Pain is very real. Some of us live every day with our thoughts, words, and actions being determined by pain. That pain could be very fresh or the result of something that happened forty years ago. It could have been caused by one major event or a series of events. It could be the result of some outside force and action or come from within our own heart and mind. Either way, the pain is alive in us.

There are several truths about pain. First, pain distorts our view of reality. It causes us to see things darkly and negatively. Second, in some cases, pain causes us to isolate ourselves. We turn away from God and others even though drawing close to God and others is just what we need. Third, pain sometimes causes us to lash out at others. Hurt people hurt people. Pain that is not transformed will often be transmitted. Our own pain always touches others around us because their lives are linked with ours. It may not affect them in the same way, but it will affect them.

We begin to overcome these monsters with a true and honest appreciation of the reality that we live in and with a new vision and experience of the presence of Jesus with us. I've heard people tiptoe around God in prayer, trying to find the right diplomatic words. They act as though if they don't say the right thing, God will ignore them or reject them. Not so!

Over and over again, especially in the Psalms and Prophets, we see how the people of God lamented over the pain they were in. As they suffered, they cried out to God in brutal honesty. They held nothing back. We must do the same. As God's children, precious and dearly loved, we need his enduring presence and the promise that he will be with us. That assurance begins with our honesty before God.

As we cry out, we must also remember to look to Jesus. It's critical that we take an honest look at him as we are taking an honest look at ourselves. Hebrews 4:14–16 is very clear about the suffering and pain Jesus endured, stating,

> Since we have a great high priest who has ascended into heaven, Jesus the Son of God, let us hold firmly to the faith we profess. For we do not have a high priest who is unable to empathize with our weaknesses, but we have one who has been tempted in every way, just as we are—yet he did not sin. Let us then approach God's throne of grace with confidence, so that we may receive mercy and find grace to help us in our time of need.

Don't miss what this is saying about Jesus understanding our weaknesses, because it is the reason we can hold fast to our faith and continue to pursue a holy life even as we suffer. Jesus willingly left heaven and came to earth for us. He came in love, knowing what the future held for him. Jesus also experienced everything that we have experienced or will experience in this life. He knows our suffering. He knows what it means to be tempted. There is no monster that Jesus didn't have to wrestle with. Yet Jesus did not sin, but gained victory over sin and suffering for us.

Jesus is the evidence of just how far God is willing to go to demonstrate faithful love for us. Because Jesus willingly took the punishment and abandonment that we deserved for our sin, God will never abandon us. That is true even when we cannot feel his presence.

Don't misunderstand me; our feelings of abandonment are real, but it doesn't mean that we are really abandoned. God will never abandon us. As Hebrews 13:5 reminds us, God said, "Never will I leave you; never will I forsake you." That is God's promise, to stand beside us in our suffering. Knowing that we are not alone does not make the pain go away, but it does take away some of its power.

Not only that, but Jesus' own life gives us the example and the type of words we can use to cry out to God. Just look at what Jesus declared in the garden right before his arrest and especially at his words from the cross.[1] He echoed Psalm 22, just one of the many psalms that illustrate Jesus' suffering and can give voice to our own.[2] The Book of Lamentations is also helpful. The very words of the Scriptures, some even from Jesus' own lips, can give us words to articulate the pain of life's worst moments. They can keep us honest, and they can also keep our vision of Jesus and his enduring presence with us clear.

---

1 See Matthew 26:36–46; 27:46; Mark 14:32–42; 15:34; Luke 22:39–46; 23:34, 43, 46; John 19:26–30.
2 Psalms 44; 60; 74; 79; 80; 85; 88; and 90 are a few others.

How important is it to remember in the midst of your suffering that Jesus knows and understands all you are going through? Why?

_____
_____
_____

How can you cultivate a habit of being more open and transparent with God, knowing he already understands your struggles and extends his grace?

_____
_____
_____

How can the confidence we have in approaching God inspire us to be honest in other areas of our lives, such as with friends, family, or colleagues?

_____
_____
_____

What I'm hearing God say to me

Study Day 4

To overcome the monsters of suffering, we need to merge honesty with a spirit of thanksgiving. I understand that when we are hurting, this is difficult to even conceive of, let alone do. Suffering destroys our perspective. We focus so much on the pain of our suffering that we fail to see anyone or anything else. That's why it is critical to not only be honest about our pain, but also to see clearly that Jesus is with us even in the midst of our pain. Only then can we begin to get a more complete perspective and develop the necessary spirit of thanksgiving.

We already know that God has invited us to cry out to him. We know that we are safe being honest with God and that, in fact, honesty is necessary in order to slay the monsters we wrestle with.

Paul's words express a spirit of thanksgiving in the midst of this honesty. He wrote, "The Lord is near. Do not be anxious about anything, but in every situation, by prayer and petition, with thanksgiving, present your requests to God. And the peace of God, which transcends all understanding, will guard your hearts and your minds in Christ Jesus" (Philippians 4:5–7).

We know that God is at hand. He is present, active, and working in history to fulfill his eternal plan in the course of time. As a result of that, Paul told us not to be anxious about anything. Instead, with a spirit of thanksgiving, we should freely make our requests known to God. When we do this, God will grant us peace—peace from the suffering and even peace in the midst of the suffering.

When Paul brought up anxiety, he was not thinking of a medical condition. Anxiety here is the enemy of the spirit of thanksgiving. To be clear, we're not talking about a deep concern for a real need in ourselves or others, including the reasons we suffer. As long as those concerns keep Jesus in the center and our responses God-honoring, then they are not the anxiety Paul was writing about.

When Paul addressed anxiety, he meant those concerns that remove Jesus from the center of our lives and, instead, place our anxiety over our sufferings at the center. That destroys our perspective and makes being truly honest about our suffering or developing a thankful spirit impossible. This is why we must take our requests to God. He, not our suffering, must be in the center, or we will never have peace.

As we take our requests to God, we don't do so like someone flailing desperately in the wind. We do so out of a heart grounded in the holiness of Jesus. We know who he is and what he has done for us. We know the wondrous salvation he has granted us even when we didn't deserve it. We increasingly know the depth of his graciousness and mercy toward us. We know more and more the richness of his love toward us. Knowing all that, we can even begin to recount the wondrous blessings he has granted us throughout our lives, including right now in our present suffering.

Recounting these truths changes our hearts and forms a spirit of thanksgiving in us. And we have to be thankful before we make our requests to God because God's love and blessings are the basis for everything. All that we are and all that we have is from him. So, without that spirit of thanksgiving for God's past and present faithfulness, our requests to God don't make any sense. After all, why would we have any confidence asking him for anything unless we knew that he was faithful and worthy of our thanksgiving?

It's only as we thank God that our requests lead to peace. That peace is not just a vague concept or a feeling. It is not just focused on some future hope, although that is part of it. This experience of peace transforms us now; it changes our hearts and minds. As pastor David Martyn Lloyd-Jones said, "If God has done the supreme thing for us in the death of His Son upon the Cross He cannot forsake us now, He cannot leave us half-way, as it were. So the peace of God that passeth all understanding keeps our hearts and minds through, or in, Christ Jesus. In that way God guarantees our peace and our freedom from anxiety."[1] This peace is a gift from God, but it is a gift that must be appropriated by us in order to be experienced. Thanksgiving is a big part of doing just that.

This peace with God is not a denial or avoidance of reality. We already know that because we have been brutally honest with God about our suffering. This peace with God is a supernatural reality that produces an inner calm and equilibrium despite the circumstances of life.

This peace with God is not the absence of fear, either. Instead, it is a sense of having our souls firmly placed in God's hands. In fact, this peace with God is so real that, no matter the circumstances, we are able to live by God's power lifting us over and through even the most difficult realities of life.[2]

This peace, which is the result of a spirit of thanksgiving, changes us and our perspective about our suffering. It does this even if it doesn't change the reality of our suffering, by bringing us deliverance. Indeed, it gives us the ability to pray, knowing that "God will either give us what we ask or give us what we would have asked if we knew everything he knew."[3] When we can thank God for who he is and what he has done, the Holy Spirit begins to grant us the peace that we need in order to transform our perspective on suffering, if not the reality of it.

The monsters of suffering are further overcome with our faithfulness before God. There is a reason oranges won't grow in Michigan, and there is a reason

---

[1] David Martyn Lloyd-Jones, *Spiritual Depression: Its Causes and Cures* (London: Harper Collins, 1965), 270.
[2] Adapted from Keller, *Walking with God Through Pain and Suffering*, 296–298.
[3] Timothy Keller, *Prayer: Experiencing Awe and Intimacy with God* (New York: The Penguin Group, 2014), 228.

cherries won't grow in Texas. The environment and the soil are inadequate. The right fruit has to grow in the right soil and climate. This is also the case with faithfulness. Faithfulness is an easily admired aspect of a holy life. However, when we are suffering, it can be a difficult crop to harvest.

When we are suffering, there seem to be all kinds of reasons not to be faithful to God. That is why we already stressed honesty and thanksgiving, which provide the right soil to harvest faithfulness. You cannot be faithful to God without them. Faithfulness itself is not rocket science, but it isn't easy, either. It means consistently pursuing the holiness of Jesus, even in the midst of our suffering and not just when it is over.

Just because we go through a season of suffering doesn't mean God takes a break in making us more like Jesus—just the opposite, in fact. During times of suffering, God is busy calling us to growth and maturity in him.

Suffering changes the way we look at ourselves. Our sense of invincibility and prideful dependence on ourselves is stripped away when we suffer outside of our control. Suffering helps us to see what is really important. When things are going well, it's easy to get caught up in very trivial pursuits, but suffering has a way of stripping those away. Suffering forces us to look to God and become dependent upon him. When all the supports of our life crumble away, we are forced to put our trust in the only true support that matters.

But there is something else suffering does that we often miss or don't think of: Suffering is almost always present in the life of any person who is used by God in great ways. It's out of those times of suffering that God makes it possible to identify with the needs of others in ways we simply couldn't before.

Indeed, I know more examples of this than I could ever count.

When my friend Harold showed up for worship less than twelve hours after his wife died, his presence was neither a denial of her death nor a denial of the reality of his grief. He was simply making clear, with his actions as well as his words, a testimony of his hope and trust in God. Faithfulness to continue to worship God in the midst of suffering is more faith-filled, hopeful, and even victorious than it looks.

When my mom continued to volunteer week after week at her local crisis pregnancy center, in the food pantry of her church, and with their cards ministry to the sick and shut-ins, she was not ignoring the reality of the debilitating and never-ending arthritis pain. She was simply displaying a consistent testimony of hope and trust in God. It is very easy to serve God when things in your life are bright, warm, and sunny. In fact, it's easy to develop an attitude that good things are happening because of your good conduct. Of course, faithful service in good times matters, but faithful service in suffering says so much more.

When my friend Marc prayed and talked from his hospital bed about the future for his life and the lives of his kids after his wife's tragic death in a terrible accident, he wasn't glossing over the pain of losing her. He wasn't ignoring the huge challenges he was going to face as a single dad to three small kids. He was simply giving voice to an emerging testimony of hope and trust in God. Perseverance is needed in our times of success because we have to remind ourselves that what we have is a blessing and not our doing. When suffering comes, though, perseverance takes on a whole new level of importance. Perseverance in times of suffering holds us together and makes it clear that we are faithful to God because we love him, not just because of the things he blesses us with.

When the people of damaged and destroyed churches across the Gulf Coast reached out to extend compassion and care after Hurricane Harvey, it was not a denial of reality or of the overwhelming needs around them. Their ongoing commitment to the ministry of the gospel and the mission of the Kingdom was a testimony of hope and trust in God. Professor Joe Bankard puts it this way:

> Compassion asks us to go where it hurts, to enter into places of pain, to share in brokenness, fear, confusion, and anguish. Compassion challenges us to cry out with those in misery, to mourn with those who are lonely, to weep with those in tears. Compassion requires us to be weak with the weak, vulnerable with the vulnerable, and powerless with the powerless. Compassion means full immersion in the condition of being human. As the church begins to embody real compassion, it is literally transformed into the loving presence of God for a hurting world.[4]

Satan, who uses suffering to try and defeat us, is defeated himself every time we serve God seemingly in exchange for nothing, especially in times of suffering. That is true when we worship, minister, persevere, show compassion, and so much more. The walk of faithfulness, especially in the midst of suffering, becomes the action that slays the monsters.

How is it possible for you to be thankful and faithful in the midst of suffering?

_____
_____

If you are able to remain thankful and faithful, how might this change your perspective on your experience?

_____
_____

---

[4] Joe Bankard, "Displaying Genuine Compassion: Spiritually Transforming the World," in *Spiritual Formation: A Wesleyan Paradigm*, 177–178.

How can your thankfulness and faithfulness even encourage those around you?

What I'm hearing God say to me

week 5 day 4

Study Day 5

Whether or not the monsters of suffering are slayed in this life, Christians live with the ultimate hope that we will overcome with Christ in the end. No one in his or her right mind looks to suffer, but when suffering comes, Christians can be defiant in the midst of it because we know where our ultimate power and hope come from. We know that God will either deliver us from our present suffering now or take us to be with him and deliver us for eternity one day. That is how Christians bear an insult without returning one. It's how we can continue to share the gospel despite being rejected or mocked. It's the only way we can endure injustice, betrayal, and persecution. We live with victory assured.

Because of this assurance of victory, we can declare with Paul, "For me, to live is Christ and to die is gain" (Philippians 1:21). That kind of declaration is not something we make lightly. We do it because we know we have only one life to live, and we don't want to waste it. We do it because the singular focus and passion of our lives is to have Jesus take full ownership of us. We want to live for something that matters now and will continue to matter in a billion years—Christ! As a result, Jesus becomes more and more visible in every area of our lives.

If we are going to die, the question is, "How can we die in such a way that, in our dying, Jesus is glorified and visible in us?"[1] That's what it means to experience death as gain. Death will reveal what our true treasure is. It will show the value of Christ in our hearts. Christ will be praised in our death if he is prized above life itself. If we learn to face death like this, we won't waste our lives.

A life that counts for eternity doesn't happen by accident. It happens when we discipline ourselves to live now, knowing that what we do has eternal consequences. It's a heart issue. Our love for Jesus is greater than our love and desire for holding on to our money, protecting our time, or refusing to risk loving and sacrificing for others. We overcome because we want Jesus more than we want to keep our lives.

If we live, the question is, "How can our life be lived to glorify Jesus at all times, even in the midst of our pain?" The way we honor Christ in life is to die to ourselves and treasure him above life's gifts. The life of a Christian includes many deaths. We are always dying to the old, to the self, to sin, to something for the sake of Christ. We sacrifice our lives so others come to know Jesus and grow in him. If we learn to live like this, then we won't waste our lives.

We'll have a new heart and mind. The world is not impressed when Christians look and act just like everyone else—always on the edge of anger, being jealous of what someone else has, speaking unkindly or impurely about others, refusing to forgive,

---

1 Adapted from John Piper, *Don't Waste Your Life* (Wheaton, IL: Crossway, 2009), 66.

or acting proud or arrogant. The world takes notice when we die to the old ways and take up genuinely new ones.

We'll have a transformed relationship with our stuff. The world is not impressed when Christians get rich and thank God. It isn't impressed when we get rewarded and thank God. It is impressed when we give away our riches and rewards for Jesus' sake and count that loss as true gain.

We'll have a transformed relationship with our time. The world is not impressed when we're always too busy or make excuses or find a way to just serve ourselves. It notices when we serve others rather than demand to be served.

And we will praise God even in the midst of pain. The world is not impressed when people talk about being faithful to God when everything is going great and they don't have a care in the world. It notices when people cling to Jesus and say, in the midst of their pain, "The Lord gave and the Lord has taken away; may the name of the Lord be praised" (Job 1:21).

A life that glorifies Jesus doesn't happen by accident. It happens when we surrender our lives to him. It's a heart issue. We want to know God, to see God, to experience God. We overcome because nothing is off limits to him. He is our life. He is our joy.

There's one more truth about overcoming because of the assured victory we have in Christ. Paul said, "We do not lose heart. Though outwardly we are wasting away, yet inwardly we are being renewed day by day. For our light and momentary troubles are achieving for us an eternal glory that far outweighs them all. So we fix our eyes not on what is seen, but on what is unseen, since what is seen is temporary, but what is unseen is eternal" (2 Corinthians 4:16–18).

Any serious reader of the New Testament knows that Paul faced immense suffering in his life and ministry.[2] So how could Paul say such things? Because he knew the sufferings of this life, no matter how bad they were, would be limited to this lifetime. That made the sufferings of this life last but a blink of an eye compared to eternity; he knew something very heavy was coming.

The coming glory of God is so heavy that even the severest of sufferings are light as a feather by comparison. More than that, from an eternal perspective, Paul knew that every ounce of pain and suffering we experience now is somehow connected with an eternal weight of glory for us. With that knowledge, we walk as overcomers, even in the midst of our suffering, because of our assured victory in Jesus.

Jesus overcame so we can overcome. Because Jesus overcame for us, we know that one day all suffering will end. Our heavenly reward is greater than anything we can ever imagine. There will be no more class division, racism,

---

[2] See 2 Corinthians 11 for one summary he gave.

sexism, or any other -ism. There will be no more political battles, recessions, terrorism, or war. There will be no more betrayal, brokenness, or disease at all. There will be no more storms, freak accidents, or unexpected tragedies of any kind. All the monsters will be slayed and all suffering will be gone for good. Here is how John described it in Revelation 21:1–7:

> I saw "a new heaven and a new earth," for the first heaven and the first earth had passed away, and there was no longer any sea. I saw the Holy City, the new Jerusalem, coming down out of heaven from God, prepared as a bride beautifully dressed for her husband. And I heard a loud voice from the throne saying, "Look! God's dwelling place is now among the people, and he will dwell with them. They will be his people, and God himself will be with them and be their God. 'He will wipe every tear from their eyes. There will be no more death' or mourning or crying or pain, for the old order of things has passed away."
>
> He who was seated on the throne said, "I am making everything new!" Then he said, "Write this down, for these words are trustworthy and true."
>
> He said to me: "It is done. I am the Alpha and the Omega, the Beginning and the End. To the thirsty I will give water without cost from the spring of the water of life. Those who are victorious will inherit all this, and I will be their God and they will be my children.

Jesus overcame so we can overcome. Our full redemption is real. Suffering and evil will one day be at an end, and our eternal rest will be assured. All of creation will be caught up in this wonderful work of God. Then, face to face with him, we will experience his indescribable glory. Jesus overcame so we can have all this. Now, in Jesus, we can overcome.

But what about today?

Charles Naylor is a spiritual hero of mine, although he died long before I was born. He was a leading hymn-writer and speaker in the Church of God movement based in Anderson, Indiana, with a huge ministry. He was in demand all over the country. Then he was involved in two terrible accidents. First, a large tent pole fell on him at a camp meeting where he was speaking. Not long afterward, he was involved in a car accident. The combination of both of those events left him almost completely paralyzed and bedfast.

Naylor was in great pain, both physically and emotionally. His public ministry ground to a halt.

People came to him and prayed over him for healing. They were close friends who knew him well and even total strangers who were moved by news of his plight. Naylor had been involved in seeing so many others restored through prayers of healing, but for some reason God did not elect to heal him.

When Naylor wasn't healed, rumors began to spread that it must have been due to some lack of faith. Others said it must be because there was some secret sin in his life. Naylor denied both and made it clear that he believed God was very present with him in his suffering. In one of his books written after the accidents, he said, "Pain is God's chisel with which he carves his image in the heart."[3]

Charles Naylor knew and experienced what we have been discussing in this chapter: God is present in our pain. He even uses our pain to build the character and holiness of Jesus in us and, in so doing, will grow us in honesty, thanksgiving, faithfulness, and hope.

Here is another testimony to the overcoming power of Jesus, from Naylor's pen:

Whether I live or die,
Whether I wake or sleep,
Whether upon the land
Or on the stormy deep;
When 'tis serene and calm
Or when the wild winds blow,
I shall not be afraid—
I am the Lord's, I know.

When with abundant store
Or in deep poverty,
And when the world may smile
Or it may frown on me;
When it shall help me on
Or shall obstruct my way,
Still shall my heart rejoice—
I am the Lord's today.

When I am safe at home
Or in a foreign land,
When on an icebound shore
Or on a sunlit strand;
When on the mountain height
Or in the valley low,
Still doth He care for me—
I am the Lord's, I know.

Nothing shall separate
From His unbounded love,
Neither in depths below
Nor in the heights above;
And in the years to come
He will abide with me;
I am the Lord's, I know,
For all eternity.[4]

Naylor was never delivered from his suffering in this life, but he definitely overcame it "by the blood of the lamb and the word of his testimony."

Perhaps God will deliver us from our suffering in this life. If he does, may we use that deliverance to bring more glory to him. But if he never delivers us from our suffering in this life, may Jesus' holiness shine even brighter in us still. Because Jesus overcame, every one of us can overcome.

---

3 C. W. Naylor, *When Adversity Comes* (Prestonsburg, KY: Reformation Publishers, 2012), Kindle location 428.
4 Charles W. Naylor, "I Am the Lord's, I Know," from *Worship the Lord: Hymnal of the Church of God*, 639.

How should our ultimate belief about overcoming at the end determine our actions in the present?

_____
_____
_____

What would help you to be "renewed day by day," and what practical steps can you take to experience this daily renewal?

_____
_____
_____

How does the promise of "eternal glory" outweigh the difficulties we face in this life? How does this truth encourage you to keep going?

_____
_____
_____

What does it take for us to allow God to use our pain to produce the holiness of Jesus in us?

_____
_____
_____

What I'm hearing God say to me

WEEK 6
True Holiness Cannot Remain Just with You

Study Day 1

In 2011, my wife, Julia, and I were privileged to join a group of other pastors to travel to Berlin, Germany, and meet missionaries whom we support there. It was a wonderful experience, the first time either of us had ever been to Europe, and the first time we got to interact personally with the exciting ministry that was happening in Berlin.

While we were there, we kept seeing bits of damage to the facades of many of the buildings throughout the city. They looked like bullet holes and char marks, and they were on all kinds of different buildings in nearly every section of the city. I knew there had been a tremendous battle in Berlin in the last days of World War II, but that was in 1945—sixty-six years prior. The damage couldn't be from that, could it?

It was.

During the war, Berlin suffered greatly. Heavy Allied bombing reduced much of the city to rubble. Street-to-street and house-to-house fighting added to the damage. By the time the war ended, virtually every structure in the city had suffered some kind of damage. Either the roof was gone or the floors and walls were severely damaged or gone. In many cases, all that was left was the facade of the building.

Now this is the really interesting part to me.

If this happened in the U.S., the building would likely have been dynamited or bulldozed and then reconstructed from scratch. But that is not what the Germans did. In many cases, they kept the old facade and rebuilt the inside. They literally remade the building from the inside out. So now, even with some of the scars from the past lingering and visible, the building itself has been transformed and made new.

Instead of being completely destroyed, the building was transformed into a restaurant, a shop, an office, or an apartment. Something that was dead was given new life. Something that was old was made new. Something that was wounded and broken was healed and made whole. What is left is a small reminder of what once was, but that has been eclipsed by the life of what now is and will be.

What a wonderful image of the gospel! The word *gospel* literally means "good news." In our context, we are talking about the good news about Jesus Christ. **In and through Jesus' life, death, and resurrection, God makes us right with him for the good of others and the world.**

Here are three ways the apostles Paul and Peter described gospel transformation:

> When you were dead in your sins and in the uncircumcision of your flesh, God made you alive with Christ. He forgave us all our sins, having canceled the charge of our legal indebtedness, which stood against us and condemned us; he has taken it away, nailing it to the cross (Colossians 2:13–14).

If anyone is in Christ, the new creation has come: The old has gone, the new is here! (2 Corinthians 5:17).

"He himself bore our sins" in his body on the cross, so that we might die to sins and live for righteousness; "by his wounds you have been healed" (1 Peter 2:24).

As you can see, the gospel states that in Christ we are made spiritually alive, with forgiveness and canceled debts. We are new creations in every way, with the old passing away and the new coming on. We once were alive to sin, but now we are alive to righteousness. This is the good news of Jesus being played out in the context of every person who belongs to him.

The gospel directs our devotion to Jesus. It's not a bunch of do's, don'ts, and opinions, but a cause worthy of our lives.

The gospel forms our relationships. It brings about mutual love, forgiveness, and reconciliation to bind people together.

The gospel changes the way we pray. Without the gospel, we're just praying to a seemingly angry, absent, or nonexistent God, but with the gospel we are praying to a God of perfect and holy love.

The gospel opens our lives up to God's supernatural power, which changes lives and circumstances.

The gospel transforms us into generous givers, with a generosity that comes from a radically regenerated heart.

The gospel stirs gratitude in us. God's saving grace and forgiving love make us grateful worshipers.

The gospel gives us eternal hope. This life is not the end, but only a shadow of the wonder that is to come.

The more we are in Christ, the more we find that the gospel is not just the *ABCs* of Christianity, a checklist we need to complete. No, the gospel is the heart of Christianity, encompassing every area of our lives inside and out.

The renewed architecture of Berlin is also a wonderful image of what the Holy Spirit continues to do as we are made holy in the image of Jesus. Or, as Paul wrote in the closing words of Galatians 6:17, "I bear on my body the marks of Jesus." Then in Colossians 1:21–23 he wrote, "Once you were alienated from God and were enemies in your minds because of your evil behavior. But now he has reconciled you by Christ's physical body through death to present you holy in his sight, without blemish and free from accusation—if you continue in your faith, established and firm, and do not move from the hope held out in the gospel."

Even the prophet Ezekiel echoed this transformation, proclaiming, "I will sprinkle clean water on you, and you will be clean; I will cleanse you from all your impurities and from all your idols. I will give you a new heart and put a new spirit in you; I will remove from you your heart of stone and give you a heart of flesh. And I will put my Spirit in you and move you to follow my decrees and be careful to keep my laws" (Ezekiel 36:25–27).

Because we are now covered in the righteousness and holiness of Jesus, we are blameless and above reproach. Indeed, we now miraculously have a new heart and a new spirit. God is giving us new purity, new passion, new power, and a new partnership.[1] Remember, *holiness is the work of God in us whereby Jesus takes full ownership of our lives, purifies us from sin, and sets us apart for his service.* These are some of the marks of that new life.

Of all the things the gospel does in a person's life, which stands out as the most impactful to you right now? How have you changed as you have grown spiritually?

_____
_____
_____

Why is a person's personal testimony of conversion such a powerful witness to Jesus and the gospel?

_____
_____
_____

Why is a person's present testimony of Jesus' Lordship just as important or even more important than her or his past conversion story?

_____
_____
_____

---

1 See Jimmy Davis, *Cruciform: Living the Cross-Shaped Life* (Adelphi, MD: Cruciform Press, 2011), 74.

What I'm hearing God say to me

Study Day 2

We live with the assurance that we are reconciled to God, that our sin has been paid for on the cross, and that we are now lovingly accepted by God, by grace alone and through faith alone. We now stand before God, covered in the righteousness and holiness of Jesus, which is giving us a new purity that we never had before. With new passion, we have a deep desire to please God with our lives. This means we want to obey his Word, saying the things Jesus would say and doing the things Jesus would do if he were walking in our shoes.

With new power, we have a growing assurance that we "have sufficient strength both to will and to do what God calls" us to do.[1] As we discussed with the *yes* position (Week 3), we must have our surrendered will merged with the ongoing grace of Jesus and the power of the Holy Spirit. Finally, in this new partnership, we are now engaged in God's mission. As Paul said, "All this is from God, who reconciled us to himself through Christ and gave us the ministry of reconciliation" (2 Corinthians 5:18). We are his servants now, and we joyfully will be bringing glory to him for all eternity.

That means that Jesus calls us, as his holy people, to be distinct *from* the world *for* the world. Our new purity, passion, power, and partnership make us different from the rest of the world around us. We are holy and being made to reflect Jesus' holiness more and more. This means we are increasingly filled with the love and glory of God. Not only that, but also our hearts are being oriented outward and not inward. This outward move is driven by the impulse of our new and increasing love for other people and our desire to glorify God with our lives no matter what the cost may be.

Maybe the simplest summary of the gospel is given to us in John 3:16–17, which states, "God so loved the world that he gave his one and only Son, that whoever believes in him shall not perish but have eternal life. For God did not send his Son into the world to condemn the world, but to save the world through him." As we have considered, our sin separated us from God. It was a breach too big for us to fix, so we were doomed to perish. However, God loved us despite our sin. Despite knowing us at our worst, Jesus came on purpose to pay the penalty for our sin. He took the punishment we deserved so we could get the life he deserved. Now all who believe in him, meaning those who give their life to him, have the promise and experience of being in an eternal relationship of love with God. God's purpose in Jesus was to make a new people, holy unto him, for his glory.

---

1 See Walter Marshall, *The Gospel Mystery of Sanctification*, revised into modern English by Bruce H. McRae (Eugene, OR: Wipf and Stock, 2005), 36–38.

First Peter 2:9–10 describes what we are like as a new people: "You are a chosen people, a royal priesthood, a holy nation, God's special possession, that you may declare the praises of him who called you out of darkness into his wonderful light. Once you were not a people, but now you are the people of God; once you had not received mercy, but now you have received mercy." First Peter also reminds us that we are holy.[2] We now relate to God in a brand-new way. We used to be outside of God's kingdom and not a people. Now, we are on the inside of God's kingdom and we are his own chosen people. Once, we had no purpose. Now, our purpose is to glorify God with our lives. Once, we were in danger of God's wrath. Now, we are recipients of his great mercy.

First Peter also describes how Christians are to relate to other people. As a holy nation, they are God's "set-apart ones." This means they are radically different from the world around them. They are God's light in a dark world. They are God's guide to a world that is lost. As a royal priesthood, they are God's "go-betweens." They minster to other people on God's behalf. Even more so, they stand as a bridge between people and God. They are deeply involved in the world around them because they know that people see and meet God through them.

What does it do in your heart and mind to know that you are one of God's people now?

_____

_____

_____

How can you be a "set-apart one" and a "go-between" at the same time?

_____

_____

_____

It's not uncommon for Christians to think of themselves as different *from* the world, but what does it mean to be different *for* the world's benefit?

_____

_____

_____

---

2 See 1 Peter 1:15–16.

What I'm hearing God say to me

Study Day 3

As Christians who are distinct *from* the world and *for* the world, we are not the same as the wider world around us. We are not the same because we belong to Jesus. He makes us holy. Being increasingly filled with his love and glory, we naturally take on a very different character. That new character can clearly be seen throughout our lives.

There are countless ways this is spelled out in the Scriptures, but perhaps the best one is through the various "one another" passages scattered throughout the New Testament. They tell us how it can be clearly seen that we are not the same because we:

- …**love** one another,[1]
- …are **devoted** to one another,[2]
- …**honor** one another above ourselves,[3]
- …live in **harmony** with one another,[4]
- …**accept** one another,[5]
- …**encourage** one another,[6]
- …**serve** one another,[7]
- …**bear with** one another,[8]
- …are **kind** and **compassionate** to one another,[9]
- …**submit** to one another,[10]
- …**forgive** one another,[11]
- …**teach** and **admonish** one another,[12]
- …**offer hospitality** to one another,[13]
- …and are **humble** toward one another.[14]

---

1 John 13:34, 35; Romans 13:8; Hebrews 13:1; 1 Peter 1:22; 3:8; 1 John 3:11, 23; 4:7–12.
2 Romans 12:10.
3 Romans 12:10.
4 Romans 12:16.
5 Romans 15:7.
6 2 Corinthians 13:11; 1 Thessalonians 5:11; Hebrews 3:13; 10:24–25.
7 Galatians 5:13.
8 Ephesians 4:2.
9 Ephesians 4:32.
10 Ephesians 5:21.
11 Ephesians 4:32; Colossians 3:13.
12 Romans 15:14; Colossians 3:16.
13 1 Peter 4:9.
14 1 Peter 5:5.

This is, of course, not an exhaustive list. However, it begins to illustrate how we have been changed from our old existence. We are not the same.

In another critical passage, Peter wrote, "In your hearts revere Christ as Lord" (1 Peter 3:15). We are not the same because Jesus is our Lord, but just saying "Jesus is Lord" is too easy. Merely mouthing the words "Jesus is Lord" does not make you a Christian. Neither does saying you believe in Jesus, knowing biblical information, or attending church services.

We are not talking about Jesus being a verbal Lord, but a ruling Lord. The words, principles, and character of Jesus affect everything we say, think, and do (as in the "one another" passages above). There are no limits! Jesus has our hearts. Our focus and passion is to know Jesus and glorify him. Whoever has our heart has the authority, and authority matters.

A couple of years ago, the post holding up my mailbox rotted out and collapsed. It needed to be replaced. The problem was that I have very little construction ability. I had no idea on my own how to install a new post, so I watched a video about it on YouTube. It looked pretty easy. So I went to Home Depot, bought everything I needed, and then proceeded to follow the video until the work was done.

In case you were wondering, it didn't take the thirty minutes the YouTube guy said it would, but after about ninety minutes I got the job done. If you send a letter to our old Texas house, it's going to go into that mailbox. The YouTube guy was the authority on that job. But when the worst that could happen is the loss of a few bucks and a couple hours of time, authority isn't really that important.

When I was laying in the pre-op area getting ready for back surgery, everyone on the surgical team kept coming in to introduce themselves and ask me different questions. I'll never forget the anesthesiologist. He said my neurosurgeon was down the hall watching what to do on YouTube!

He was obviously joking, but can you imagine putting whether or not you will be paralyzed for the rest of your life in the hands of a guy learning what to do from a YouTube video? When your life is on the line, authority matters a whole lot more.

If Jesus is Lord, then he is the ultimate authority in our lives. We know who Jesus is and what he wants from us because he has revealed it to us through God's Word, the Bible. When we read it, the Holy Spirit speaks to us and guides us into all truth. In so doing, the Lord Jesus has our heart, and we are consistently not the same as the wider world around us.

When we set apart time to worship and grow spiritually with other Christians, it stands out. When we hold our tongue rather than lashing out, it stands out. When we seek to understand rather than pre-judging someone else, it stands out. When the world is so used to sexist, racist, or demeaning talk, and we are inclusive, kind, and gentle, it stands out. When we don't curse or speak in coarse ways as others do, it stands out. When we are honest and trustworthy while others lie, it stands out. When we protect the ones everyone else picks on, it stands out. When we try to bring reconciliation and peace instead of joining in the criticism and gossip, it stands out. When we give generously rather than think of ourselves first, it stands out. When we are quick to say sorry when we are wrong, it stands out. And when we stand out in these ways, people see how impossible the difference is without Jesus and how we are truly not the same.

Because we are not the same, the world will see how we endure personal loss for heavenly gain. Opportunities abound to honor and glorify Jesus, but almost all of them require you to lose something first. That's the risk. Every person we know who is far from God will be reached for Christ only at the cost of our personal loss. It's a risk because it will take our money, our time, our hospitality to strangers, and, most of all, a love beyond our comfort zone.

Finally, because we are not the same, we will have to be both firm and soft. On the one hand, we must be firm in our commitment to Jesus, obeying him at all costs, even when it's hard.

Rebecca Manley Pippert shares a story of a Christian law student who came up to her after a talk she gave at a Christian college convention. He confessed, "Look, I cheat on my exams, and I feel kinda guilty about it. But I figure it's all right because I really want to be a lawyer for Christ."[15]

Clearly, something was mixed up in this student's understanding of what it means to be a Christian. But he was not alone. There are all kinds of ways we compromise what we know to be true and right for the sake of expediency or ease. And the truth is that if we are not firm in our commitment to Jesus in small things, we will fail to be firm in big things, as well. The world is watching. It may be stunned by our firm commitment, but it will take note and see Jesus in our lives at the same time.

On the other hand, our love and compassion for people must be soft. A local pastor told me about a woman in his congregation whose husband left her. She didn't want to come to church because she was so embarrassed. She knew someone would ask about him, and she didn't want to answer. However, at the pastor's urging, she came. Within minutes, someone did ask about her husband. Immediately, her lips quivered. But before words came out of her mouth, that person hugged her and wept with her. They sat together in worship, and the woman's secret was eventually revealed. However, rather than judging her or shunning her, the church rallied around her and lovingly supported her that day and throughout one of the toughest seasons of her life.

---

15 Pippert, 179.

week 6 day 3

You see, if we won't be soft in our love and compassion for others, people will miss seeing Jesus in our lives. And the world is watching. It may be stunned by our soft hearts toward others, but it will take note and see Jesus in our lives, too.

Every time we are living what we say we believe about Jesus, we will not be the same. Our thoughts, words, and actions will be different from the world around us. As a result, we may heighten the world's curiosity about Christianity, force it to have to think through and wrestle with what it is seeing in us, and hopefully cause it to seek Jesus for itself. It's about being God's "set-apart ones" (holy nation) and his "go-betweens" (royal priesthood).

Take the "one another" passages listed above. Which of them has most touched your life personally when you saw it on display? What was the impact?

_____
_____
_____

Why is the failure to live out the "one another" passages so destructive to our witness?

_____
_____
_____

Pick one or two of the "one another" passages you feel are most needed in the circles you run in. Why would practicing them stand out so clearly?

_____
_____
_____

What I'm hearing God say to me

Study Day 4

As Christians who are distinct *from* the world and *for* the world, we will not be silent. In fact, when we are not the same, we won't even have the chance to be silent. Now we need to look at the second half of what Peter said earlier. Writing to a church under trial and threat of persecution, he said, "Always be prepared to give an answer to everyone who asks you to give the reason for the hope that you have. But do this with gentleness and respect, keeping a clear conscience, so that those who speak maliciously against your good behavior in Christ may be ashamed of their slander" (1 Peter 3:15–16). We will be people who say what we live.

Being "prepared to give an answer" means that we must live questionable lives. This does not mean questionable in terms of odd or inappropriate. It means questionable in terms of being distinctly different and compelling.

A life of holiness has been, is, and always will be a "questionable" life. It means speaking about who Jesus is and what he has done for us. It means being clear and directed. We are trying to persuade people to put their faith and lives in Jesus as we have. He is our ultimate hope, after all. So, our words don't communicate pat answers or meaningless platitudes but instead describe our experience about the eternal hope we have in Christ. After all, "What we have to offer others is not a life of rigid self-consciousness but a life of joyful abandonment to God. Life lived this way is the most powerful magnet for evangelism there is."[1]

Evangelism is a word Christians are familiar with, but they often know more about what it isn't or shouldn't be than what it is or should be. On the negative side, they may think of some obnoxious person on TV, or someone with a bullhorn or a bunch of tracts on a street corner. On the positive side, they may think of Billy Graham preaching to huge crowds, a Campus Crusade leader giving a focused gospel presentation to a student, or someone taking a missions trip to a foreign country.

Either way, most of us wrestle with what evangelism is and what kind of role we are to play in it. Unfortunately, much of the time we think of it as a hard sales pitch forced on someone else.

In a story that illustrates our dilemma about evangelism, Pastor Kevin Harney tells about a woman who would daily force-feed her dog a tablespoon of castor oil. The dog would always run and hide because he knew what was coming. Someone had told this woman that the daily castor-oil regimen would be good for her dog's health. So every morning, she pinned her beloved dog down, forced his mouth open, and poured the castor oil in. The woman did not enjoy this process, and neither did her dog.

---
1 Ibid., 139.

Then one day, the dog managed to kick the bottle of castor oil out of the woman's hand, and it spilled all over the floor. The woman went to grab a towel so she could clean up the mess. But when she returned, she found her dog happily licking up the spilled castor oil. The woman laughed because it all made sense now. Her dog actually liked castor oil; he just hated having it forced down his throat.[2]

Christians should not force-feed Jesus to anyone. The simple truth is that true holiness cannot be contained in us; it must be shared. And if we live questionable lives, people will be attracted to Christ. We believe in faith that the Holy Spirit will do that work. And, as people are attracted to Jesus through what they see in our lives, they will ask us to "give the reason for the hope that we have."

This brings us to another powerful word, from 1 John 3:16: "This is how we know what love is: Jesus Christ laid down his life for us. And we ought to lay down our lives for our brothers and sisters." Because we have received the love of God, it is only natural that we share that love with others. We are not the same. In light of what Jesus has done to lay down his life for us, it is only natural for us to lay down our lives for others. It's what we do as we pursue this life of holiness.

Observing and experiencing that love over time will naturally cause others to question us. Here is what I mean:

- We can **restore** an elderly woman's fence.
- We can **redeem** a neighborhood park for kids.
- We can **forgive** someone's debt to us.
- We can **provide** for the needs of someone who lost her or his job.
- We can be **hospitable** to a stranger in church by inviting that person to lunch.
- We can show **compassion** to someone who is sick by visiting her or him.
- We can speak in ways that are **pure** and **build up** rather than in ways that are impure and tear down.
- We can try to broker **peace** in the midst of a conflict of our own or between others.

Jesus would do each of these things if he were in our shoes. Such moves are risky because there are no guarantees as to what the response will be, but we know they honor Jesus.

---

[2] See Kevin G. Harney, *Seismic Shifts* (Grand Rapids: Zondervan, 2005), 253–254.

Would you characterize your life as one of "joyful abandonment"? If so, how so? If not, why not?

_____
_____
_____

How is displaying our joy as a testimony to God's presence and work in our lives possible regardless of our personality type (for example, even for an introvert)?

_____
_____
_____

Why is what we do in Jesus' name just as important as what we say about him?

_____
_____
_____

How can God use you to live a radically different life before others so you are clearly not the same as everyone else?

_____
_____
_____

week 6 day 4

What I'm hearing God say to me

Study Day 5

How we live matters. It's a powerful part of our witness. And what we say matters, too. God calls us to offer a verbal testimony of his work in our lives when we have the opportunity. But in both cases, it is critical that we are pointing to Jesus and not to ourselves. Our attitude must be like that of John the Baptist, who said of Jesus, "He must become greater; I must become less" (John 3:30). Jesus must take center stage in our words and our actions.

If Jesus is becoming greater and we are becoming less, then we are leading questionable lives. We will not be the same and, because we are not the same, we will not be silent. People will ask why. And when they ask why, we have the opportunity to "give the reason for the hope that we have."

Every time we answer someone's questions this way, we are becoming less and Jesus is becoming greater. We are making him, not us, the hero of the story. We don't know where the conversation will go from there or what will happen next. We don't know what the person will say or do, but we will know for sure that we are living as God's "set-apart ones" (holy nation) and his "go-betweens" (royal priesthood).

Just like the buildings in Berlin, our outward appearance doesn't change after we become a Christian. We typically have the same career, possessions, personality, and interests. Yet we are not the same. The difference is that now we hold loosely to all of those things and cling tightly to Jesus and the mission of his Kingdom.

We often still have some evidence of the scars left behind from our life before Christ. Yet now those scars are no longer a reflection of the shame of our past. Instead, they are increasingly becoming a sign of the change that has occurred and the beauty of our transformation in Christ. We have been made holy by Jesus and are increasingly being filled up with the love and glory of God. As a result, we can't be silent. The love and glory of God that are filling our lives naturally spill out of us on everything and everyone we encounter.

I lived in Texas, a state full of cattle ranches (one is even bigger than the entire state of Rhode Island). Most ranches in the U.S. have fences to mark their boundaries. Those fences determine who is allowed in and who must be kept out. However, that is not how things are usually done in Australia, another place filled with cattle ranches. In Australia, their ranches are often so large that fencing everything in would be too expensive and impractical. This means cattle can easily roam on and off of the ranch and get mixed in with the cattle from another ranch.

So, what do the ranchers in Australia do?

They bore a hole deep into the soil and create a well of precious, life-giving, life-sustaining water. In the Outback, as in any arid place, water is a matter of life and death. Having dug that important well, the Australian ranchers can then assume that, although some cattle may stray, they will never go too far from the well. As long as there is a supply of clean water, the livestock will remain close.[1]

The gospel is like one of those life-giving wells. As Jesus makes us holy and we are renewed in the image of Christ, we need that living water of the gospel to sustain us. Not only that, but we also need the power of the gospel to make us distinct from the world, for the world. And when that happens, we will not be the same, and we won't be silent, either. Seeing us, others will want to drink from that well, and we will be used by God to lead them to it.

We all know instinctively how *not* to evangelize because we've seen some pretty bad examples. So, what is the right way to do it?

_____
_____
_____

Why is what you say about Jesus just as important as what you do in his name?

_____
_____
_____

How can you do better at not staying silent when an opportunity to speak about Jesus comes up?

_____
_____
_____

---

[1] Adapted from Jim Belcher, *Deep Church: A Third Way Beyond Emerging and Traditional* (Downers Grove: InterVarsity Press, 2009), 86.

What I'm hearing God say to me

WEEK 7
There's No Such Thing As Personal Holiness without Social Holiness

Study Day 1

Martin Luther King Jr. is widely quoted as having said, "Most people are thermometers that record or register the temperature of majority opinion, not thermostats that transform and regulate the temperature of society."[1] Too often those words prove true, but that doesn't have to be the case.

The year 1963 was an explosive time during the civil rights movement throughout the American South, a movement that was primarily given voice and energy by the black church. This was especially true in Birmingham, Alabama. As blacks called for desegregation, equal rights, and access to opportunity, some whites responded with brutality; many blacks were beaten or jailed or even had their homes bombed. It was so severe that one black section of Birmingham became known as "Dynamite Hill."[2] With all that was going on, there was every reason to back down, stay safe, and play by the rules of injustice as many had before.

But many blacks in Birmingham couldn't back down any longer. King explained it this way:

> Only a Negro understands the social leprosy that segregation inflicts upon him. Like a nagging hound of hell, it follows his every activity, leaving him tormented by day and haunted by night. The suppressed fears and resentments and the expressed anxieties and sensitivities make each day of life a turmoil. Every confrontation with the restrictions is another emotional battle in a never ending war. He is shackled in his waking moments to tiptoe stance, never quite knowing what to expect next. Nothing can be more diabolical than a deliberate attempt to destroy in any man his will to be a man.[3]

Willing to stand against injustice, King and others led march after march for equality. Despite their justified anger and rage, they marched non-violently, willing to suffer the consequences. At one point in the Birmingham struggle, King and other leaders were arrested on a trumped-up charge, as a way to "present our bodies as a personal witness in this crusade."[4] It was Good Friday.

A few days later, from his jail cell, King wrote a letter to white ministers. In his "Letter from Birmingham Jail," King laid out a biblical philosophy of nonviolent resistance to injustice and evil. He called out the church for remaining "silent behind the anesthetizing security of stained glass windows."[5] He challenged it, saying, "If today's church does not recapture the sacrificial spirit of the early church it will lose

---

[1] Brenda Salter McNeil, *Roadmap to Reconciliation 2.0* (Downers Grove: InterVarsity Press, 2020), 138.
[2] See Stephen B. Oates, *Let the Trumpet Sound: A Life of Martin Luther King, Jr.* (New York: Harper Perennial, 2013), 227.
[3] Ibid.
[4] Ibid., 232.
[5] Martin Luther King Jr., "Letter from a Birmingham Jail [King, Jr.]," accessed March 6, 2025, https://www.africa.upenn.edu/Articles_Gen/Letter_Birmingham.html.

its authenticity, forfeit the loyalty of millions, and be dismissed as an irrelevant social club with no meaning for the twentieth century."[6]

King pleaded with the church's heart through sentences such as, "Injustice anywhere is a threat to justice everywhere."[7] Then he called the church to action by embracing the charge of being an extremist for love, as Jesus was. He said, "So the question is not whether we will be extremists, but what kind of extremists we will be. Will we be extremists for hate or for love? Will we be extremists for the preservation of injustice or for the extension of justice?"[8]

Days later, King was released—and he went right back to leading the marches personally. He led adults as well as children. As they marched, they were arrested, fire hoses were turned on them, dogs were released, and some people were beaten. This happened day after day—and still they marched. Over all the chaos, King cried out,

> We must say to our white brothers all over the South who try to keep us down: We will match your capacity to inflict suffering with our capacity to endure suffering. We will meet your physical force with soul force. We will not hate you. And yet we cannot in all good conscience obey your evil laws. Do to us what you will. Threaten our children and we will still love you.... Say that we're too low, that we're too degraded, yet we will still love you. Bomb our homes and go by our churches early in the morning and bomb them if you please, and we will still love you. We will wear you down by our capacity to suffer. In winning the victory, we will not only win our freedom. We will so appeal to your heart and your conscience that we will win you in the process.[9]

This powerful, Christ-centered call for justice permeated King's life and the movement he led.

And then the forces of evil and injustice cracked.

On May 5, 1963, Reverend Charles Billups was leading a column of children down the street toward a line of police dogs, fire hoses, and armored cars. The police commissioner, a hateful man named Bull Conner, was calling out from a megaphone, telling them to turn back. The marchers knelt in prayer, then sang, and then prayed again. Here is how King biographer Stephen Oates told the story:

> Suddenly Billups stood and confronted the police. "We're not turning back. We haven't done anything wrong. All we want is our freedom.... How do you feel doing these things?...Bring on your dogs. Beat us up. Turn on your hoses. We're not going to retreat." Then he started forward, followed by the other ministers and the children. Connor whirled about and yelled,

---

[6] Ibid.
[7] Ibid.
[8] Ibid.
[9] Oates, 252.

"Turn on the hoses." His men just stood there. "Damnit! Turn on the hoses!" But as the blacks marched through their ranks, the firemen and cops fell back "as though hypnotized." Some of the firemen were crying. The Negroes continued their journey unimpeded, prayed for their imprisoned comrades in front of the jail, then headed back to the Negro section singing "I Got Freedom Over My Head."[10]

It took many more days to gain victory over segregation in Birmingham and the rest of the American South. But that moment was powerful! That's what it looks like when injustice is overcome in a way that reflects the holiness of Jesus.

When I first read this story, I couldn't help but feel simultaneously heartbroken and inspired. It breaks my heart that a fight such as this even had to be fought. It breaks my heart that the church of Jesus Christ as a whole was not completely united in this fight, especially as clear-cut as the justification for this one was. But I am also inspired because those marchers, most of them committed Christians, were thermostats for the cause of Christ. The courage they showed in the face of evil inspires me. The commitment they had to the values and tactics of Jesus, when it would have been so easy to match the tactics of their oppressors, inspires me. Their actions were changing the temperature for justice and righteousness in and around them. Their cause was a holy one.

Most of us want to be identified with being part of a holy cause such as that from the vantage point of history. It's easy to join the struggle when it's all over and won. Missiologist Ed Stetzer says,

> Quoting Dr. King [in our day] is good, helpful, and insightful, yet it is hardly the same thing as standing with him in 1963. His principles have not changed, but the climate in which we quote him has. We look back on those who publicly stood up for the civil rights movement during this period with respect and admiration, precisely because of their sacrifice. If we want to emulate that kind of love, it goes beyond merely quoting them in the safety of historical retrospect but to speaking out on the same issues, which often remain unpopular today.[11]

Being part of a holy cause for justice counts the most when you are right in the middle of the struggle, with challenges to face and costs to be paid and the outcome of the battle still in doubt.

While some of the circumstances have changed over time, the struggle against the evils of injustice remains. As a people, we are clearly still wrestling with racial injustice. We are not what we once were, but if the events of recent years have taught us anything, we are not yet what we can be and should be. Not only that,

---

10 Ibid.
11 Ed Stetzer, *Christians in the Age of Outrage* (Carol Stream, IL: Tyndale, 2018), 226–227.

the recurring questions around poverty and immigration cry out for answers that change the hearts of individual people as well as the public policies of state and national governments.

The same can be said for the cause of life and the cause of peacemaking.

We don't need more "thermometer Christians," just reflecting the temperature of the majority opinions of the circles they run in. Thermometer Christians are merely followers of culture. They reflect the culture's selfishness, hypocrisy, divisiveness, unforgiveness, and injustice. Instead we need "thermostat Christians" who change the temperature of the culture for good. They bring on selflessness, generosity, integrity, unity, forgiveness, mercy, love, and justice. The circles they run in are different because they are there, and that difference reflects the holiness of Jesus.

The Christians in Birmingham in 1963 were thermostats. So were the Christians who accepted death rather than embrace violence in the gladiatorial games, or the ones who protected innocent and unwanted babies from infanticide in ancient Rome, or the ones who stayed behind to care for and bury the dead during the medieval plagues, or those who founded hospitals to care for the needy, or the abolitionists in England and America who helped end slavery, or the ones who founded schools to teach the poor to read and write and find a better life, or the ones who fight against sex trafficking or stand up for refugees today. They all could have easily been added to the list of the heroes of faith included in the Book of Hebrews. These heroes where the kind of Christians

> who through faith conquered kingdoms, administered justice, and gained what was promised; who shut the mouths of lions, quenched the fury of the flames, and escaped the edge of the sword; whose weakness was turned to strength; and who became powerful in battle and routed foreign armies. Women received back their dead, raised to life again. There were others who were tortured, refusing to be released so that they might gain an even better resurrection. Some faced jeers and flogging, and even chains and imprisonment. They were put to death by stoning; they were sawed in two; they were killed by the sword. They went about in sheepskins and goatskins, destitute, persecuted and mistreated—the world was not worthy of them (Hebrews 11:33–38).

The world we live in needs to see more thermostat Christians today. The church needs to see them, too. So do I. So do you.

I don't know about you, but when all is said and done on this earth, I don't want to be a thermometer Christian. I want to be a thermostat Christian. That is the heart-cry and passion of people pursuing a holy life in Jesus. Make no mistake, though; there is a cost associated with being a thermostat Christian. There always has been. There always will be. But that is exactly what God is calling us to.

From cover to cover, the God of the Bible is a God of justice; it is a key part of his character. Justice is a foundational attribute of his holiness. **Justice and holiness are linked in the identity and character of God and must be linked in the identity and character of his people.** As we have said, *holiness is the work of God in us whereby Jesus takes full ownership of our lives, purifies us from sin, and sets us apart for his service.* That means we are to have a profound effect on the evil and injustice in our world, literally taking back what hell has stolen.

Isaiah wrote, "The LORD Almighty will be exalted by his justice, and the holy God will be proved holy by his righteous acts" (Isaiah 5:16). He was linking justice and holiness in the identity and character of God.[12] Jesus himself echoed the prophet Isaiah when he described his own mission: "The Spirit of the Lord is on me, because he has anointed me to proclaim good news to the poor. He has sent me to proclaim freedom for the prisoners and recovery of sight for the blind, to set the oppressed free, to proclaim the year of the Lord's favor" (Luke 4:18–19). Justice is everywhere in God's Word.

There are four key ingredients to biblical justice: distribution, power, equity, and rights. Overall, a holy God demands that his holy people be concerned to equally distribute society's goods and rewards, while also equally applying punishments and penalties as they are deserved. That is where we get the notions of both social justice and criminal justice.

At the same time, a holy God demands that his holy people exercise power legitimately. Power should be used to maintain equity and the rights of others. In other words, a holy God demands that his holy people be fair and balanced toward those who are like them as well as those who are not. They are to resolve conflicts and treat people fairly in all respects.[13]

Here is how theologian Chris Marshall sums it up:

> Holiness is not simply a case of ethnic distinction, of being separated from other nations as God's chosen people…. Nor is it primarily a matter of observing prescribed religious rituals. *The essential mark of holiness is a lifestyle of justice.* Just as "the LORD of hosts is exalted by justice, and the Holy God shows himself holy by righteousness", so, too, God's people are to reveal their set-apartness by their passion for justice…. For holiness means wholeness as well as separation. It describes a life of completeness and unity and goodness, a life that reflects God's own integrity and self-consistency, a life that is animated by justice.[14]

---

12 See also Isaiah 58:1–14; Amos 5:21–24; and Micah 6:6–8 as other wonderful examples of God's overall character and commitment to justice.
13 See Christopher D. Marshall, *The Little Book of Biblical Justice* (Intercourse, PA: Good Books, 2005), 31.
14 Ibid.

Living in this way, with a passion for holiness and justice, will make you a thermostat Christian.

Doing justice has both micro and macro expressions. In a micro sense, individual Christians, pursuing a holy life in Christ, will act justly and seek justice in their personal lives and social networks. That will have a profound effect on the *shalom* they experience and also bring to others (remember Week 4). However, in a macro sense, groups of Christians pursuing life in Christ will act justly and seek justice corporately, which should have a profound effect on families, churches, neighborhoods, communities, and entire cultures.

In other words, if we are pursuing holiness in Jesus, the fruit of that holiness never stays with us (remember Week 6). Doing justice always ripples out to affect others, those who need justice restored to them and those who need to be in the restoration business with us. Not only that, but when we join with God's collective people to do justice, the possibilities to touch others for the glory of God become endless.

Why does the Bible link justice and holiness so many times?

_____
_____
_____

Why is the subject of justice usually seen as a political issue rather than a biblical one? How can Christians change that mindset?

_____
_____
_____

Where is a place of injustice that God has caused to capture your heart?

_____
_____
_____

In your walk with Jesus, how have you been a thermometer or a thermostat when it comes to biblical justice and holiness?

_____
_____
_____

What I'm hearing God say to me

Study Day 2

Now let's make what we are talking about very concrete and practical.

As we pursue a holy life under Jesus, we will have a growing desire to see the most vulnerable receive justice. Echoing so many other Bible passages, Zechariah 7:9–10 states, "This is what the Lord Almighty said: 'Administer true justice; show mercy and compassion to one another. Do not oppress the widow or the fatherless, the foreigner or the poor. Do not plot evil against each other' "[1]

When Zechariah mentioned widows, the fatherless, foreigners, and the poor, he included the most vulnerable people in the society of ancient Israel. Those people were the easiest to exploit, the most likely to be abused, the most frequently ignored, and the easiest to justify animosity toward. Not much has changed today.

Zechariah made it clear how God commands the vulnerable ones to be treated. True judgments are to be rendered. In other words, no cheating or exploiting people. Kindness and mercy should be shown. Love and hospitality should be extended. No one should be oppressed, and no evil should be planned against them. That will guarantee that they have equal opportunity and a life without fear of harm.

Those commands were basic, but God's people repeatedly forgot them, ignored them, or just outright rebelled against them. That is why the Lord chastised them over and over. Their lack of justice to the vulnerable was a key sign of their sin and their abandonment of God. It shows that they were thermometers, reflecting the temperature of the wider culture of the nations around them rather than thermostats that changed the temperature by loving the things and the people God loves.

Jesus made care for the vulnerable a key characteristic of life in his Kingdom. In the Parable of the Sheep and the Goats, he said there will be a clear separation between those who care for the vulnerable and those who don't. The sheep will care for the vulnerable, in effect caring for Jesus personally. In so doing, they will be bringing glory to God. And at the judgment, Jesus will tell them, "Truly I tell you, whatever you did for one of the least of these brothers and sisters of mine, you did for me" (Matthew 25:40).

At the same time, the goats will ignore the vulnerable, and at the judgment, Jesus will tell them, "Truly I tell you, whatever you did not do for one of the least of these, you did not do for me" (Matthew 25:45). The sheep will go to eternal life, and the goats will go to eternal punishment. It doesn't get much clearer than that.

We know that we are saved and right with God by grace through faith and not by our works. We also know that we stay right with God by that same grace. However, as

---

1 See also Leviticus 19; Deuteronomy 10:18; Jeremiah 7:6; Ezekiel 22:7, 29; Malachi 3:5; James 1:27.

someone wiser than I has said, "We are justified by faith alone, but not by faith that is alone."[2] Our lives are secure because of what Jesus has done and not what we do, but if we have really received what Jesus has done, others will see it in our actions. Tim Keller contended, "There is a direct relationship between a person's grasp and experience of God's grace, and his or her heart for justice and the poor."[3] I believe this is where thermostat Christians are made.

A thermostat Christian is not motivated to care for the vulnerable out of a sense of guilt. A sense of guilt is what motivates the world to address social issues and show concern for the vulnerable, but it doesn't work, at least not in the long term. It doesn't work because we have a built-in defense against that guilt. We always have reasons to justify ignoring those in need and keeping what's ours to ourselves. There are a million different reasons, and they all seem valid. Guilt is a thermometer appeal. It only works for a short time, if it even works at all.

But grace is an appeal that arouses the heart and passion of the thermostat Christian. In a sermon preached more than 170 years ago, pastor Robert Murray McCheyne said,

> Now dear Christians, some of you pray night and day to be branches of the true Vine; you pray to be made all over in the image of Christ. If so, you must be like him in giving…"though he was rich, yet for our sakes he became poor"…. Objection 1. "My money is my own." Answer: Christ might have said, "My blood is my own, my life is my own"…then where should we have been? Objection 2. "The poor are undeserving." Answer: Christ might have said, "They are wicked rebels…shall I lay down my life for these? I will give to the good angels." But no, he left the ninety-nine, and came after the lost. He gave his blood for the undeserving. Objection 3. "The poor may abuse it." Answer: Christ might have said the same; yea, with far greater truth. Christ knew that thousands would trample his blood under their feet; that most would despise it; that many would make it an excuse for sinning more; yet he gave his own blood. Oh, my dear Christians! If you would be like Christ, give much, give often, give freely, to the vile and poor, the thankless and the undeserving. Christ is glorious and happy and so will you be. It is not your money I want, but your happiness. Remember his own word, "It is more blessed to give than to receive."[4]

Out of the realization that they are recipients of the abundant, life-giving grace of God, thermostat Christians are aroused to the just cause of the vulnerable. They respond in micro ways through whatever means they have, and they join with all of

---

2 I've seen this quote attributed to John Owen, John Calvin, and Martin Luther.
3 Timothy J. Keller, *Generous Justice* (New York: Penguin Books, 2010), Kindle location 191.
4 Robert Murray McCheyne, Sermon LXXXII, in *The Works of the Late Rev. Robert Murray McCheyne*, Vol. 2 (New York: Robert Carter, 1847), 479. I found this quoted in John Piper's book *Don't Waste Your Life* (Wheaton, IL: Crossway, 2009), 165.

God's people to act in macro ways to address the issues of justice through public policy, community partnerships, and direct action on behalf of the wider church.

The thermostat Christian knows there will be resistance along the way and many costs to pay. Resistance is to be expected. And responding to needs and bearing burdens is inherently costly. Raising the issues of the vulnerable often shines the spotlight on the oppressor at the same time. Sometimes that oppression is visible, clear, and indefensible, but other times it is systemic, ingrained in societies and cultures. That means people may mock us, try to dissuade us, distort our motives, or even outright attack us as we address issues of justice to the vulnerable. In the face of those costs and that resistance, thermometers will just take on the temperature of the majority, but thermostat Christians will stand strong and change the temperature, knowing they are glorifying God.

Who are the most vulnerable people in your life? How are you burdened to see them receive justice?

_____
_____
_____

How does experiencing God's grace inspire you to care for the vulnerable people in your life?

_____
_____
_____

What I'm hearing God say to me

Study Day 3

As we pursue a holy life under Jesus, we will have a growing desire for justice to overcome the evils of racism, classism, and sexism. As he wrote to the church in Galatia, the apostle Paul made it clear that those who are adopted in Jesus' love are empowered to glorify him in every arena of life. He said, "In Christ Jesus you are all children of God through faith, for all of you who were baptized into Christ have clothed yourselves with Christ. There is neither Jew nor Gentile, neither slave nor free, nor is there male and female, for you are all one in Christ Jesus. If you belong to Christ, then you are Abraham's seed, and heirs according to the promise" (Galatians 3:26–29). That passage is nothing short of earth-shattering in any context, but it is especially so in the context of the Roman empire of the first century.

Paul argued throughout Galatians that the promises of the Old Testament, especially the promise to bless the nations through Abraham, were fulfilled in Jesus. The Law was epitomized in Jesus. Spiritually, we are Abraham's sons because we belong to Jesus. Paul even retained the word *sons*, which makes clear that everyone—including females—is a "spiritual son" for the purpose of being adopted and inheriting the wonderful blessings of life in Christ. So, in Christ we are all equally children of God and joint heirs of all of God's promises. The ultimate promise of God, though not explicitly addressed in Galatians 3 and 4, is experienced in his Kingdom, a place of holiness under Jesus' rule and reign.

The Kingdom is not just something for the future, where nothing that happens now matters. We are not just on this earth to survive injustice until the future comes. And the Kingdom is not just for now, with no hope for God's future and ultimate victory. The Kingdom is both now *and* future. There is a role God calls us to play now, and there is a guarantee of his final victory in the future.

One day all racism, classism, and sexism will be gone for good. However, every time we fight against those evils now is a sign of that ultimate victory to come in the future. And the church of now is supposed to be a clear and visible example of what the Kingdom will look like in the future.

Because we are heirs of everything in God's kingdom, things are now different in that place where the Kingdom should be most visible—the church. There should be no racism in here. There should be no classism in here. And there should be no sexism in here. The world may be the same as it has always been *out there*, but because of Jesus, things must be very different *in here*, in the church.

As Paul wrote to the Galatians, he knew that every nation had high spiritual walls that separated people by race. But Paul taught and lived that Jesus came and knocked those walls to the ground. So, while it is true that racism has always been present, even in the church, from the beginning God has been moving to break down all those walls to admit people from every race, tribe, and tongue. That meant that a Jew (such as Paul) would embrace a Gentile (such as Titus) or a person of mixed heritage (such as Timothy). There is simply no place for racial walls because Jesus tore them all down.

Paul also knew, as he wrote to the Galatians, that every culture had a pecking order determined by whichever class you were in. The rich, powerful, and free were at the top. The poor and the slaves were at the bottom. Paul taught and lived that Jesus came and turned that pecking order upside down. As people made in the image of God and as joint heirs with Christ, we all stand equal before him. So, while it is true that classism has always been present, even in the church, God has moved to raise up people because of who they are in Christ and not because of their status in the world. The story of Philemon and his slave, Onesimus, is just one example.

Perhaps the most radical implication Paul was making in his letter to the Galatians was that, in God's kingdom, the door was no longer closed to women. They were no longer to be seen as just wives and mothers, some kind of second-class citizens or worse. Paul taught and lived that Jesus came and opened the doors to women. So, while it is true that sexism has always been present, even in the church, God acted to move women from the outside in contemporary Roman society to the center of church life. They were founders of churches and leaders of churches. In fact, Paul's ministry often depended on the support and leadership of women such as Chloe, Phoebe, Apphia, Lydia, Priscilla, and Junia.

Whether we are talking about the culture of the Roman Empire of Paul's time or about any other time in history up to the present day, there has always been a strong temptation for thermometer Christians to simply reflect the temperature of the powerful, systemic, and sinful social structures around them. William Wilberforce, the hero of abolition in Great Britain, was especially clear about this problem. Writing to British Christians who continually made excuses for systemic sins such as slavery, he argued, "Our behavior is so conformed to cultural standards that if we were put on trial as a Christian, the case might be dropped for lack of evidence."[1]

Thermometer Christians won't necessarily engage in these evil -isms directly. They may even pat themselves on the back because they didn't utter a racial slur or publicly mock someone outside their social group or formally ban a woman from using her gifts to glorify God. The sad truth is that the thermometer Christian is blind, maybe even willfully blind, to the suffering and injustice around him or her. He or she is content to remain safe in the background, hoping the problem will simply resolve itself.

---
1 William Wilberforce, *Real Christianity*, rev. Bob Beltz (Ventura: Regal Books, 2006), 65.

To sum it up, the problem with thermometer Christians when it comes to the -isms is their ignorance and their comfortable silence. The "case" against them will be dropped because their lives reflect the cool temperature of the world more than the warmth of the holiness of Jesus.

But when a thermostat Christian is put on trial, he or she will proudly stand guilty as charged. There will be great evidence of that person's attempt to confront the sinful injustice of those -isms. That has been true of thermostat Christians such as Sojourner Truth and Desmond Tutu and the abolitionist or civil rights movements throughout history they were a part of. It was true of Dietrich Bonhoeffer and the Confessing Church that stood up for Jews against the Nazis, and of William Booth and the Salvation Army and John Wesley and the Methodists, who championed the church's ministry and inclusion of people in every social class. And it has certainly been true of countless men and women who fought against infanticide and polygamy long ago or people such as Frances Willard, who fought for women's suffrage in the nineteenth century, and Christine Caine, who fights against human trafficking today. These thermostat Christians applied the holiness of Jesus in micro and macro ways to the real problems of injustice around them, and because they raised the temperature, we felt God's warmth among us.

When it comes to life inside the church, thermostat Christians settle for nothing less than for the church to reflect the warmth and beauty of Jesus' holiness. They cringe whenever they see signs of any of the -isms in the church. They don't shrink back in ignorance or silence like the thermometer Christians. Instead, they lean into the problem. They never tolerate any racial walls, pecking orders, or closed doors in the church because they know these things represent sin, plain and simple. That is why they reach out to build relationships of mutual understanding with Christians of other races and backgrounds. They listen with compassion to the pain of the hurting. They lead the way in repentance, and they resolve to right wrongs and pursue reconciliation wherever possible. They advocate for the inclusion of people who are on the outside or who are different. Beyond that, however, thermostat Christians from every background get better and better at valuing and embracing different cultures, backgrounds, and people because that glorifies God.

Outside of the church, thermostat Christians are on the lookout for places where they can express the warmth of Christ. Thermostat Christians have the same conviction as Abraham Kuyper, who said, "There is not a square inch in the whole domain of human existence over which Christ, who is sovereign over *all* does not cry out: 'Mine!' "[2] As a result, they want to see the -isms die in their families, neighborhoods, workplaces, cities, and beyond.

---

[2] Quoted in Charles W. Colson, *The Faith* (Grand Rapids: Zondervan, 2008), 106.

While there is always a cost to standing up against the different -isms, thermostat Christians never forget that Jesus' Great Commandment calls us to "love your neighbor as yourself" (Matthew 22:39). Sometimes that neighbor is someone like us in every respect, but most of the time that neighbor is very different from us, just like the Good Samaritan.[3]

Thermostat Christians are not cold. They don't freeze up in the face of these challenges. Instead, they know that, when they live out the holiness of Jesus, "social justice gives relevance and bite to the language of Christian love."[4] That is why thermostat Christians rise up and match words of love with actions of love and justice in any place where an -ism remains, glorifying God every step of the way.

What must it be like to be a repeated victim of one of the "-isms"? If this has been the case for you, how have you been impacted by a particular injustice?

___

Where have you seen the damage of the "-isms" in the lives of others? How has this damage burdened your heart to see these -isms overcome?

___

How can you use whatever power and position God has given you be a listening ear, a comforter, or an advocate for justice to overcome the "-isms"?

___

---

3 See Luke 10:25–37. Jews and Samaritans traditionally hated each other, which is why Jesus' parable about the wide range of who our neighbors are is so amazing.
4 Richard Foster, *Streams of Living Water* (New York: HarperCollins, 1998), 178.

What I'm hearing God say to me

Study Day 4

As we pursue a holy life under Jesus, we will have a growing desire for all life to be valued and cherished. God told Jeremiah, "Before I formed you in the womb I knew you, before you were born I set you apart; I appointed you as a prophet to the nations" (Jeremiah 1:5). Later, Paul told the Ephesian church that God "chose us in him before the creation of the world" (Ephesians 1:4). What a powerful sense of assurance that God creates all life and that no living person is an accident. Some of us may be a surprise to our parents, but no one has ever been or will ever be a surprise to God.

Not only does God create all life, but he also values all life. That is clear especially throughout the Gospels. Jesus touched, loved, and blessed children, who would otherwise have been largely ignored or marginalized in that society.[1] He touched and healed those who would have been pitied or forgotten, such as the lame, the blind, and the deaf.[2] He even touched and healed the greatest social outcasts of his day, those with leprosy.[3] There was no one whose life lacked value and worth in Jesus' sight.

Sadly, however, the world we live in often devalues life in general and can even create a culture of death. There are millions of abortions each year, as well as many thousands or even millions of infanticides. There are millions of people exploited and trafficked as slaves throughout the world, some under the radar even in our own country. Beyond that, there are untold numbers of children who are abused or neglected due to poverty, addiction, disease, and abandonment. In some cases, such as in the nation of Iceland, people even brag that they have cured disabilities such as Down syndrome, when the "cure" is actually genetic testing followed by abortion.[4] We could go on and on.

Into this culture of death, Christians must follow Jesus and cry out for life. They understand that God knows us completely and is fully present with us. And they, like David, know that we are "fearfully and wonderfully made" (Psalm 139:14). That is why, from the beginning, Christians have celebrated that all life is created by God and is of great value to him. This was a remarkable position to take, especially in the Roman world. "Unlike the Romans, Christians did not hold human life to be cheap and expendable. It was to be honored and protected at all costs, regardless of its form or quality. By doing so, they countered many of the depravities that depreciated human life."[5]

---

[1] See Matthew 19:13–15.
[2] See Matthew 15:30.
[3] See Matthew 8:1–4.
[4] Stephen Camarata, "Iceland 'Cures' Down Syndrome: Should America Do the Same?" Psychology Today, accessed March 29, 2019, https://www.psychologytoday.com/us/blog/the-intuitive-parent/201801/iceland-cures-down-syndrome-should-america-do-the-same.
[5] Alvin J. Schmidt, *How Christianity Changed the World* (Grand Rapids: Zondervan, 2004), 48.

This belief drove Christians to oppose abortion and infanticide as the murder of the young and innocent and to oppose euthanasia as the murder of adults. They were driven to adopt babies that were abandoned and raise them as their own. Christians also opposed the violence and death associated with the gladiatorial games. While there have been some sad exceptions throughout history, a commitment to the sanctity of life has always been the consistent passion of Christians.

Christians are pro-life. But being pro-life is very different for a thermometer Christian and a thermostat Christian. For a thermometer Christian, pro-life simply means a political position that one only has to think about every couple of years when there is an election. Once a thermometer Christians casts his or her secret ballot, that person can then just reflect the temperature of the wider culture. In other words, being pro-life for a thermometer Christian has little or no cost, requires little or no effort, and means next to nothing in really creating a culture of life in his or her corner of the world or beyond.

A thermostat Christian is much different. Author Philip Yancey sums up the attitude of the thermostat Christian in this way: "Our confused society badly needs a community of contrast, a counterculture of ordinary pilgrims who insist on living a different way. We can make the world stop and think before pulling a trigger or exacting revenge or neglecting the vulnerable or euthanizing those it deems 'devoid of value'.... Though we will not sweep all evil from the world, we can at least present a shining alternative."[6]

For thermostat Christians, being pro-life means they live to spread a culture of life wherever they go and with everyone they are around. They declare in word and deed that all life is valuable. They remove the climate of shame that keeps pain and brokenness in the darkness. They expand the church family so no one will ever be neglected or abandoned. And they become agents of redemption.

No one I know personally has been more of a thermostat Christian for the cause of life than my mother. Before my parents even met, my mom was tragically assaulted by an acquaintance. It was 1971, she was single and in her early 20s, and she became pregnant in one of the most tragic and traumatic ways. When she went to the doctor, he encouraged her to have an abortion and try to put the pain behind her, yet something in my mom's heart knew that to do so was unthinkably wrong. An abortion would only add a new tragedy to an already tragic situation.

But being raised in a strict Catholic family meant that being pregnant and unmarried carried a lot of shame, even in a situation such as this one. So my grandparents sent my mom away to live with my uncle in another state until she was ready to give birth. When the baby was born, my half-sister Dianna was placed for adoption with a couple

---

6 Philip Yancey, *Vanishing Grace* (Grand Rapids: Zondervan, 2014), 261–262.

who could not have children of their own. They raised her, and now she is an adult with a family of her own.

That was not the end of the story for my mom. For the rest of her life, my mom was an advocate for pro-life causes of every kind. Yes, that involved her politics, but it also involved counseling teen mothers at a local crisis pregnancy center and paying the costs of time and emotional energy that went with it. She was an agent of redemption for many other women in all sorts of situations.

While my mom's story is not necessarily normative for everyone else in that circumstance, there is no doubt that, despite her personal tragedy, God helped her to be a thermostat Christian. In her corner of the world, things got warmer. And God was glorified through it all.

What is the value of life in your life?

_____
_____
_____

How has God burdened you to expand your thinking and living to be truly pro-life?

_____
_____
_____

What I'm hearing God say to me

Study Day 5

As we pursue a holy life under Jesus, we will have a growing desire for the peace of Christ to reign everywhere on earth. Jesus set the tone for peace very clearly in the Sermon on the Mount when he said, "Blessed are the peacemakers, for they will be called children of God" (Matthew 5:9). He also taught that there is a different way to resist evil than the world does, even including the command to love our enemies.[1] James 3:18 echoes this sentiment clearly, explaining, "Peacemakers who sow in peace reap a harvest of righteousness."

We don't have to look very far to see the absence of peace in our world. Just watch the evening news tonight, and you will see bullying on social media, fights breaking out at schools or in the workplace, families entangled in dysfunction, crime on display, and random acts of violence that take our breath away. Those are all localized examples where peace is missing, and there are even more on a nationwide or worldwide scale. That would include political unrest, terrorism, war, and genocide. The list is truly endless.

In this mistrusting, angry, and even violent world, Christians model the peace of Christ. They live at peace with God, and out of that peace they are able to pursue peace with others. They don't take revenge. They don't hold grudges. They build bridges of peace. They know that the work of peacemaking is hard, but they also know peace is the only real way to live and be free. It is the only way for them to make their enemies their friends.

No Christian is against peace. However, there is once again a huge difference between a thermometer Christian and a thermostat Christian. Thermometer Christians settle for the absence of open conflict. They will even call a situation peaceful when victims are pacified, distracted, or so exhausted that everything is calm. This fake sense of peace is enough for thermometer Christians to relax and look the other way, especially when they are not suffering through any personal pain or injustice. It is easy for a thermometer Christian to be lulled to sleep in a fake peace.

A thermostat Christian is not lulled to sleep so easily. Christian peace activist Shane Claiborne makes the true peace of the thermostat Christian clear:

> True peace does not exist until there is justice, restoration, forgiveness. Peacemaking doesn't mean passivity. It is the act of interrupting injustice without mirroring injustice, the act of disarming evil without destroying the evildoer, the act of finding a third way that is neither fight nor flight but the careful, arduous pursuit of reconciliation and justice. It is about a revolution

---

1 See Matthew 5:38–48.

of love that is big enough to set both the oppressed and the oppressors free.[2]

Thermostat Christians are wide awake to the need for peace all around them. Their struggle for peace may be personal on a micro-scale, but it goes beyond them to the macro-scale as well. In both scales, however, thermostat Christians work for peace, whether or not they are personally affected by evil. They resist evil without becoming the evil they resist. They don't join in evil, instead exposing it and letting the evilness of evil speak for itself. Sometimes they mock the absurdity of evil with creativity and humor. They always expose injustice with righteousness. And when it comes to peacemaking, they take the long-range view, being committed to peace no matter the cost and no matter the time it takes to get there.

One example would be the Quakers of New York and Philadelphia, who were thermostat Christians for sure. On February 11, 1790, soon after the Constitution of the United States was ratified and George Washington became president, they petitioned Congress to immediately end the slave trade.

This was a politically explosive stance to take. Slavery was one of the main obstacles to ratifying the Constitution and forming the federal government to begin with. It was clear that slavery went against the principles of the American Revolution. Even Thomas Jefferson, the principal author of the Declaration of Independence and himself a slave owner, wrestled with this obvious inconsistency. Slaves, who were considered three-fifths of a person in the Constitution, certainly didn't have access to the right to "life, liberty, and the pursuit of happiness."

These Quakers raised a question no one wanted to answer, but it was a question that demanded an answer in the cause of peace. How could one group of people, who claimed to be committed to liberty and freedom for all, do violence to another group of people by forcibly enslaving them?

The answer was simple, but the implications of that answer were not. Representative James Jackson of Georgia furiously stood up to respond. "The Quakers, he argued, were infamous innocents incessantly disposed to drip their precious purity like holy water over everyone else's sins."[3] His insult was more like an unintended compliment for the thermostat Christians they were.

The Quakers took a risky stand against slavery. They stuck out their necks to love and advocate for people they had never met. With no real clout and no real power of their own, they worked for peace in a cause that must have seemed insurmountable. It sounds like a no-brainer today, but it was very risky then. Why would they do that? For one reason alone: Jesus was first, and everything else was second. Jesus called them to be peacemakers, and so they were.

---

2 Shane Claiborne, *Common Prayer* (Grand Rapids: Zondervan, 2010), 382. I originally found this quote associated with a tweet from Idelette McVicker on July 28, 2018.
3 Joseph J. Ellis, *Founding Brothers* (New York: Vintage Books, 2000), 81.

Those thermostat Christians lost the battle that day, and they would continue to lose battle after battle for many years to come, but they took the long view, knowing that the culture was getting warmer and warmer through their struggle. Eventually they won the war against slavery and for peace, all for the glory of God.

If we want to be holy, if we want Jesus to take full ownership of our lives, then we must renounce every time we are simple thermometers, just reflecting the temperature of those around us. We need to be thermostats instead, spreading the warmth of Jesus' holiness rather than the cold of the crowd. This means we will be set apart for Jesus' loving service in the cause of justice for his glory.

Consider the words of this Franciscan benediction:

> May God bless you with discomfort at easy answers, half-truths, and superficial relationships so that you may live deep within your heart.
>
> May God bless you with anger at injustice, oppression, and exploitation of people, so that you may work for justice, freedom and peace.
>
> May God bless you with tears to shed for those who suffer pain, rejection, hunger and war, so that you may reach out your hand to comfort them and to turn their pain into joy.
>
> And may God bless you with enough foolishness to believe that you can make a difference in the world, so that you can do what others claim cannot be done to bring justice and kindness to all our children and the poor.[4]

I would add this: May you be a thermostat that raises the temperature of justice and righteousness with the warmth of Jesus' holiness in ways big and small in your life and beyond. Amen!

Where is peace most absent in your community? in your social network?

_____
_____
_____

How has God burdened you to be a peacemaker? What might the costs and sacrifices be?

_____
_____
_____

---

4 McNeil, 139.

What I'm hearing God say to me

CONCLUSION

Never forget: We are in the middle of a war, and there is no time for a fingernail inspection.

We are in a battle that is raging over who will have ultimate control of our hearts. It's a battle that is waged in our thoughts, words, and actions every day. It's a battle for the souls of men and women, boys and girls.

Yes, we are saved and made holy by grace alone, through faith alone, in Christ alone, to the glory of God alone, but we also know that holiness is something we must fight for every day.

We fight to kill sin before it kills us.

We fight to stay in the *yes* position with God.

We fight for *shalom* in every relationship in our lives.

We fight to overcome in the midst of suffering, knowing that Jesus overcame for us.

We fight to be distinct *from* the world *for* the good of the world.

And we fight for justice to be done in Jesus' name.

I have been a Christian for over thirty-five years now and a pastor for about twenty-six of them. I am more convinced than ever that God's grace and mercy are big enough for me. I am holy in Christ because he made me so. At the same time, however, I know I need to fight for Jesus' holiness to be more visible in my life.

I want to be holy. I want to be filled up with the holiness of Jesus. I want him to take full possession of my life. I want to be purified from sin and set apart for his service. I want that more than anything, but I also know that I regularly come up short in my fight for holiness.

That is why I can never forget that Jesus is my substitute. He carried all of my sin—past, present, and future—with him on the cross and paid for it once and for all. He stood in my place. Now I am forgiven and alive in him only by grace. At the same time, I am holy in him by grace, too. My substitute, Jesus, made that possible. He still does. He always will.

Let me tell you about Fred and Sally.

Fred has made lots of mistakes in his life. He's hung out with the wrong crowd for a long time. He partied hard, and he has all the scars to prove it. He's squandered his money on sinful things. He's been far from God a long time. He knows that, but others have also reminded him of it, over and over. There is no shortage of sin or regrets in his life. He is full of guilt and shame. He doesn't think he is worthy of God's love or, for that matter, of anyone else's. So many people have told him they will never forgive him that Fred assumes God is the same. He feels perpetually hopeless.

Have you ever met someone like Fred? Are you like him yourself?

The good news of the gospel is that Jesus is Fred's substitute. Fred deserved to die for his many sins, but Jesus paid the price for them. Jesus never did the kinds of things Fred's crowd did, not once. Jesus doesn't have Fred's scars of a life far from God, none. But Jesus died for Fred's sin.

When Fred responds to the gospel, he is saved and made holy by grace alone, through faith alone, in Christ alone, to the glory of God alone. That means he belongs to Jesus. Fred belongs to Jesus when the Holy Spirit works inside him to purify his heart and life from the inside out. And he still belongs to Jesus when he comes up short in his fight for holiness and parts of his old life show up again.

Fred is not perfect. But Jesus' substitution for Fred is perfect. It always will be.

I'm like Fred. I can't believe how much my old life still reappears when I get mad or when I go to places I shouldn't go. I can't believe how quickly it can happen. That's why I am so glad Jesus is my substitute. I need him so much!

Sally is the opposite of Fred in many ways. She is really good. She doesn't have any of Fred's vices. She never drank or slept around. She watches her language and hangs out with the right crowd. She manages her money well. Sally is in church all the time. The problem is that she is full of pride and constantly judges others. That pride and judgmental attitude make her bitter. She doesn't forgive people who wrong her. She holds grudges. She thinks she is superior to all of "those people," people such as Fred.

Have you met someone like Sally? Are you like her yourself?

Jesus is Sally's substitute, too. She deserved to die for her sinful pride and judgmental attitude just as Fred deserved to die for his sins, but Jesus paid that price, too. Jesus was never prideful, not once. Jesus was never judgmental, not once. But Jesus died for Sally's pride and judgmental attitude.

When Sally responds to the gospel, she is saved and made holy by grace alone, through faith alone, in Christ alone, to the glory of God alone. That means she belongs to Jesus. Sally belongs to Jesus when the Holy Spirit works to turn her pride into humility and her judgmental attitude into graciousness. And she still belongs to Jesus when she comes up short in her fight for holiness, and the pride and judgmental attitude show up again.

Sally is not perfect. But Jesus' substitution for Sally is perfect. It always will be.

I'm like Sally. I can't believe how full of pride I can get. I can't believe how superior and arrogant I can be. Sometimes it's so common that I don't even notice right away. That's why I am so glad Jesus is my substitute. I need him so much!

Jesus being our substitute is everything. Never lose sight of that.

All of life in Jesus is grace from beginning to end. That never stops. And all of life in Jesus is a fight for holiness from beginning to end. That never stops, either.

Daniel Sidney Warner was one of the fathers of my church group, the Church of God (Anderson, IN). More importantly, he was a man who was passionate for the holiness of Jesus to be on display in his life. In his journal, on April 17, 1877, he wrote these words: "Since I rose this morning my constant prayer has been to God to lead me in all things. I pray God to take me like an old sack and shake me until entirely empty, and then fill me with the fullness of God."[1]

That is my prayer for myself and for you, too. May God grant us both the grace to walk in the light of Jesus' presence today. May we be more and more emptied of the things of this world and may we be more and more filled with the things of Jesus. And may we see the slow and steady work of the Spirit shape us, our relationships, and everything around us with the clear and visible marks of Jesus' holiness. Amen!

---

1 Daniel Sidney Warner, personal journal entry, April 17, 1877.